The Art
of
Christian Listening

by

Thomas N. Hart

PAULIST PRESS
New York/Ramsey

Library of Congress
Catalog Card Number: 80-82810

ISBN: 0-8091-2345-2

Published by Paulist Press
545 Island Road, Ramsey, N.J. 07446

Printed and bound in the
United States of America

Contents

Introduction

Carl Jung, the great German psychiatrist, once remarked that everyone longs to tell his or her story to someone and have it understood and accepted.

Most of us can probably recognize that desire in our own hearts. It is an important thing to keep in mind when someone comes to us and begins to open to us his or her life-story. To listen with an attentive and receptive heart until that person is finished is to bestow a gift of great value.

Bishop Alban Goodier tells of the time he was in the seminary, and his superior came to his room one night, closed the door, and sat down and cried. He was amazed and touched that his superior should repose this kind of confidence in him, so completely letting down his guard. It was a moment of deep communion, and Goodier regarded it afterward as one of the great gifts of his life.

It works both ways. The person who tells the story bestows a gift on the listener. The person who attends and appreciatively receives bestows a gift on the teller.

There is nothing quite so sacred, so fragile, or so mysterious as the human being. There is probably no service we can render other persons quite as great or important as to be listener and receiver to them in those moments when they need to open their hearts and tell someone their story. This is the kind of conversation the present book focuses on under the heading of "helping relationships."

1

There are many kinds of helping relationships. Some are no more formal than ordinary friendships, or the relationship of parent to child. Some form suddenly and without warning, as when a neighbor, dropping in for coffee, begins to talk about a personal or family problem, and the telling contains an implicit plea for help. There are more structured helping relationships, such as students coming to teachers with other than academic concerns, clients going to professional therapists, men and women approaching a priest in the sacrament of reconciliation, wanting something more than just absolution for a trail of offenses. Priests and ministers today find themselves asked more than ever before for spiritual direction by religious and lay folks alike. A growing number of sisters are asked to serve as spiritual directors and retreat directors for their own communities and for lay people. As ministry broadens in the Church, lay people respond to requests to visit the sick and dying, work with youth in religious education and other programs, prepare young couples for marriage. As these sorts of demands increase, many feel the need for a fuller orientation to helping relationships, some definition of what the helping role is and is not, some principles to guide the effort and make it maximally fruitful.

It is not uncommon for people to shy away from such serious conversations, or to suffer them with feelings of great uncomfortableness and inadequacy. "I am neither wise nor holy. Why is she telling *me* all this?" "But he is older than I am, and better educated too! What can I possibly say to him?" "It makes me extremely uncomfortable when people cry, or when they pose questions about life I don't know the answers to myself." "I cannot and will not take responsibility for anyone else's life!" "I've got enough problems of my own, and have all I can do to keep my own head above water. Who am I to act as counselor?" These are typical human reactions to the importunities of the needy. When they determine the response, those who long to tell their story to someone turn away still burdened. A great opportunity has been lost. Parents, teachers, doctors and nurses, residence hall directors, family members, friends, even priests and ministers find themselves avoiding encounters of this kind, trying instead to cheer people up and keep it light. They thus lose the chance to engage in a very important and much needed ministry.

It is to this situation that the present work hopes to speak. It might be called a book on spiritual direction, except that that term sounds esoteric and seems to apply only to a very specific sort of exchange with a very specially qualified person. We want to speak more broadly, in such a way as to include classical spiritual direction but to embrace other kinds of Christian helping relationships as well. What we have in mind is all those one-on-one relationships in which one person is implicitly or explicitly asking another for help to grow in his or her life as a Christian human being. It may be a layperson, sister, or priest seeking an ongoing spiritual direction relationship. It may also be a student trying to find a way through adolescent growth or through delicate interpersonal relationships. It may be a person coming alive in faith and inquiring about how to begin or deepen a life of prayer. It may be a friend or neighbor trying to be responsible in a difficult marriage, or an older person facing terminal illness. The variety here is considerable and needs to be adapted to in appropriate ways. But the quest is common: What does it mean to be a Christian? How do I strengthen my relationship with God, and interact with people more as Christ would? How can I pray better, and be more Spirit-led in the important choices of my life? How can I cope with suffering and get more from it? What is Christian growth, and how do I foster it in my life? The concern does not always center around a problem. Sometimes it is nothing more specific than a desire to grow, to move beyond the place where one is to a deeper and richer place.

The purpose of the present book is to make people more comfortable with the idea of ministering to others in this way. It does this by promoting understanding. It describes the role of the Christian helper quite concretely, and tries to allay anxieties about having to be older, better educated, holier, wiser, and closer to God than the person seeking help. It shows that one need not be a mystic, a theologian, or a professional counselor to be able to assist another to Christian growth, provided only one have a basic grasp of the shape of the Christian life and the principles of human interaction. In the interest of clarity, it sets forth the objectives of helping relationships, and at the same time states their limits.

The book is laid out as follows. The opening chapter offers the basic description of the Christian helper in terms of sacramentality and earthen vesselhood. The next chapter sets out the basic roles involved: that of the person seeking help, that of the helper, and that of the Lord. Then there is a discussion of the difference between the Christian helper or spiritual director and the psychological counselor. A chapter on the lineaments of Christian growth sets forth the objectives of the relationship, and prepares the way for a treatment of two particularly important areas: prayer and Christian choices. The next chapter names some of the pitfalls of the helper. Then there are a number of suggestions on how to prepare oneself for this ministry. Two chapters describe concretely the typical sorts of situations the helper deals with. The book closes with a summary of the many ways in which people seeking help return the blessing to the helper.

1. Helper as Sacrament

Roman Catholics have been brought up with the idea that there are seven sacraments, each a channel of grace, each, on a more recent presentation of the matter, an encounter with Christ. This is true and important. Each of the seven sacraments is a meeting with God, the deepening of the relationship, an increase in life. The unfortunate byproduct, however, of a concentration on ritual sacraments as the time of the encounter with God is that it diverts attention from all the other encounters and experiences of God's grace, the ones which have no names and come to us unsought and unprepared for. We go to church to find him, and wait for the "real presence" and communion. Our spirituality would be much richer if we realized that these are only some of the ways God meets us. If God is alive and well, interested in his world, and present to it at all times and places, if he is a God who is always disclosing himself and offering himself for relationship, then we may be in a communication situation much more than we usually imagine.

The Second Vatican Council has formally broadened the notion of sacrament in the church, endorsing an emphasis which has become increasingly dominant in theological reflection. Returning to a notion of sacrament as old as the Fathers of the Church, the Council calls attention to the fact that there are two levels of sacramentality more basic than that of the ritual sacraments. Christ is the primordial sacrament. The church is the next most basic sacrament. Then come the seven ritual sacraments, derivatively.

Christ is a sacrament because he incarnates God and reveals him. "He who sees me sees the Father" (Jn 14:9). Incarnation and sacrament are the same idea: an invisible reality finds a visible embodiment, and what is transcendent comes to us in matter. God is the great mystery beyond our grasp; in Christ, we touch him. We hear his word, feel his care, experience his faithfulness, know his compassion and his mercy. Thus Christ is the primordial sacrament.

> That which was from the beginning, which we have heard, which we have seen with our eyes, which we have looked upon and touched with our hands, the word of life . . . we proclaim to you (1 Jn 1:1–3).

Next comes the church. The church is not a building or a great many buildings. These are places where the church gathers. The church is not a hierarchy and a priesthood. These are individuals within the church who provide an important service. The church is all God's people. The images employed by Vatican II to set forth the mystery of the church are the dominant biblical images: People of God, Sheepfold, Body of Christ, Bride of Christ, Branches of the Vine. They are people images, organic, and they are the most original descriptions of the church we possess. What they point up is a truth we have sometimes forgotten, taking the part (the hierarchy) for the whole: that the church is the community of all those persons who belong to Christ.

Vatican II calls this community of persons a sacrament (*Constitution on the Church,* #1). The designation may seem odd, but its explanation is found in the basic notion of sacrament already considered. Like Christ, Christians incarnate something and bring it to visibility. What we incarnate is Christ, and that is why we are called the body of Christ. For Jesus of Nazareth is no longer present as an individual on the stage of history, as he was for a limited period of time in the first century. He died, and has undergone transformation into a glorified state. His incarnation in the world now is the church, all those human beings who have been baptized into him and breathe his Spirit.

Let us be concrete and experiential about this sacramentality of Christians. Why were the slaves who came in off the slave ships to Cartagena in the seventeenth century, sick, lonely, afraid, sometimes near death, so moved when they came into contact with Peter Claver? Because he incarnated the love and ministry of Christ. Why are the dying poor in Calcutta's streets so moved and uplifted by their contact with Mother Teresa and her sisters? Because they incarnate the love and ministry of Christ. Why do we respond as deeply and strongly as we do to our contacts with a really good priest or minister, whether that encounter be ritually sacramental or not? Because his presence, his words, his relation to us so unmistakably carry Christ's own presence and activity. Why do some people say they experience God more profoundly on a beautiful Sunday morning in a backyard brunch with their family than they do in going to church? Why do others testify that a dinner with a close friend over life's important questions is more of a religious experience for them than the Eucharist often is? Is not this too because there is a kind of pervasive sacramentality in the world which bears God to us, so that when we touch the depths of any experience we touch him? Well, is there any more compelling bearer of the holy than the human person made in God's image and likeness in the first place, and, as a Christian, striving to put on Christ? This is the root of the church's sacramentality.

Here we have the explanation of a very important saying of Jesus:

> Jesus answered them, "Destroy this temple, and in three days I will raise it up" ... But he spoke of the temple of his body. When therefore he was raised from the dead, his disciples remembered that he had said this, and they believed the scripture and the word which Jesus had spoken (Jn 2:19–22).

In the Old Testament, the temple was the holy place, God's own house. This saying of Jesus about destroying it naturally got him into trouble with the religious authorities, and they used it as evidence against him in his trial (Mk 14:58). For by these words he signifies nothing less than a religious revolution. God's temple is no longer a building, but Jesus' body. This is the holy place now, the place of the encounter with God. That might be easy enough for us Christians to accept, believing as we do in the divinity of Christ. But have we adverted sufficiently to the meaning of his body? What is his body? During the life of the historical Jesus, it is his own person. But the passage speaks explicitly of his resurrection. After his resurrection, his body is the church. The early Christians built no churches, but broke bread in their homes (1 Cor 11:17-34). It was in one another that they met, reverenced and served God.

> Do you not know that your body is a temple of the Holy Spirit within you, which you have from God? (1 Cor 6:19).

> Now you are the body of Christ and individually members of it (1 Cor 12:27).

> Truly, I say to you, as you did it to one of these, the least of my brothers or sisters, you did it to me (Mt 25:40).

> Saul, Saul, why do you persecute me? (Acts 9:4).

> The person who receives you receives me, and the one who receives me receives him who sent me (Mt 10:40).

If we really grasped this sacramentality of the Christian community, it would make an immense difference to our spirituality.

Helper as Sacrament

Now let us look specifically at the helping relationship in the context of the church. We are social beings; none of us makes it alone. Where the genesis and nurture of our faith are concerned we depend vitally on that community of persons who are grounded in the same faith experience. Though our prayer be often solitary, and the responsibility for our life ultimately our own, we do not deal with God in a vacuum, but in the context of a human community. At certain times, especially, we feel the need of someone's help. What do we find when we seek it? Just another human being? No. If the church is sacramental, if human beings, in the Spirit of Jesus, are the sacrament of God's presence and action in the world, then we meet more than the person whose assistance we seek. The encounter is sacramental. It does not matter whether the helper is ordained or not, or whether the transaction is an officially acknowledged ritual sacrament or not. The invisible is somehow present in the visible.

Out of this comes the helper's most basic self-understanding. Any helping relationship in the context of Christian faith is a mysterious encounter. God is somehow present and at work in it. What the helper is doing goes beyond his or her powers and his or her deliberate intent. He or she does everything possible, uses all available personal resources, thinks and acts as if everything depended on him- or herself. At the same time he or she knows that all of this is just a vehicle for something larger than itself, whose operation is hidden and unsearchable, whose influence goes beyond the means at hand and even the ends sought. The work of the helper is in this respect like the work of the preacher. We know what we say and we know what we mean. But what God may be saying in our words to any given hearer is a matter quite beyond our calculation or control. It makes sometimes for the greatest surprises.

> To him whose power at work in us is able to accomplish
> more than we could ask or even conceive, to him be glory
> in the church and in Christ Jesus, now and forever. Amen.
> (Eph 3:20).

The helper can properly regard him- or herself as making God present to the other in God's concern, compassion, acceptance, support. People need that. God can seem very distant, and oneself very much alone. God may well be believed in, but there is no real experience of him. He is a notion, not a reality perceived. And then comes incarnation. At the hands of someone in a helping role, a person sees flesh and blood on a lot of faith notions. God is real, is present, does care; his word heals, his assurance gives strength, his faithfulness is life. Through the experience of being ministered to by one who shows a genuine personal concern, an acceptance which goes beyond one's deserts, and an affirmation of all that is good in one's life, a person can believe, perhaps for the first time, that God is love and what he is said to have said is true. The helper takes one seriously, and implicitly expresses the confidence that one can take responsibility for one's own life and turn it to some account. This gives the person the exultant feeling that God himself is holding out life as something precious, and offering a person his or her selfhood as a gift and charge of immense value.

The importance of incarnation or sacramentality to our life with God can hardly be overestimated. In the Old Testament, when God called the prophet Samuel as a young boy, Samuel did not know what he was dealing with or how to read the communication. He needed the help of an older man schooled in God's ways to confirm and clarify his vocation (1 Sam 3). The advice the old man, Eli, gave was that Samuel should say, when he felt the Lord calling, "Speak, Lord, your servant is listening." When he did that, the Lord's message came clear to him. Many is the person since who has been confused about the way God was dealing with him or her, and found clarity only in talking it through with someone else who shared the faith and knew something of God's ways.

It is instructive to note how much Jesus uses the sacramental principle in his ministry, particularly where healings are concerned. Over and above the sacrament of his own historical personality, he uses all sorts of material media for the action of God. He lays his hand on the leper (Mk 1:41), puts his fingers into the ears of the deaf and dumb man and touches his tongue with spittle (Mk 7:33), tells the blind man to go wash in the pool of Siloam after he anoints his eyes with clay (Jn 9:7), tells the ten lepers to go show themselves to the priests (Lk 17:14). He can heal at a distance without any apparent instrumentality, but even there it is his word, accepted in faith, that effects the cure (Jn 4:40). Thus it is typically in some sacramental or materially mediated way that Jesus gives new life to individuals. This is God's accommodation to humanity, for we are body-persons. John Henry Newman noted long ago that we are influenced much more by what is concrete and immediate than by what is abstract, even if it is logically reasoned. All religions are aware of it, having their sacred times, sacred places, sacred objects, sacred persons. The sacramental principle is God's way of dealing with us, making the invisible visible, the inaudible audible, the intangible tangible. In a helping relationship in the context of faith, sacramentality is the key to understanding its mysterious efficacy.

Beset with Weakness

This could be misunderstood. The helper somehow embodies the presence of Christ, yet may lack many of the virtues of Christ. The helper's words somehow carry a word of God to the other person, but the helper should never confuse his or her words for those of the Lord. The helper may be able to do quite remarkable things for people, but should never allow him- or herself to be puffed with pride at the ownership of such great power.

Perhaps it is precisely to make such mistakes difficult that God typically gives the helper a profound feeling of inadequacy and personal poverty. The title of Henri Nouwen's book, *Wounded Healer*, perfectly expresses the paradox. Because this is such a common experience, it merits consideration.

We usually think of St. Paul as the epitome of personal strength and self-assurance. Not only does he take strong theological positions and state them with uncompromising boldness; he takes on both the multitudes and the powers that be with indomitable courage. Add to this his testimony of extraordinary religious experiences in his conversion and his visions and revelations, and you have the picture of a man who apparently lies prey to no doubts, and cannot be turned aside from his objectives either by difficulty or penalty. Yet it is this Paul from whom we have the words: "We have this treasure in earthen vessels, to show that the transcendent power belongs to God and not to us" (2 Cor 4:7). It is Paul who writes:

> To keep me from being too elated by the abundance of revelations, a thorn was given me in the flesh, a very messenger of Satan, to keep me from being too elated. Three times I besought the Lord about this, that it should leave me; but he said to me, "My grace is sufficient for you, for my power is made perfect in weakness" (2 Cor 12:7–9).

It is not difficult to find ourselves in this portrait. We too have thorns in the flesh, and would love to be without them. They bother us, and often they seem to impede our effectiveness in doing God's work. We often feel our weakness, the fragility of an earthen vessel carrying a treasure on which it has far too vulnerable a hold. Sometimes this becomes quite acute, as people press on us with their many needs, and we search our souls wondering what we shall give to them: "There is a lad here who has five barley loaves and two fish; but what are they among so many?" (Jn 6:9). We can never extricate ourselves from the embarrassing position of fellow struggler, seeker, sufferer. Sometimes our woes seem too great to allow us to look up from them and open ourselves to the pains of another. Well, Paul has apparently felt this too. He describes himself as hanging on by a thread at times:

> We are afflicted in every way, but not crushed; perplexed, but not driven to despair; persecuted, but not forsaken; struck down, but not destroyed (2 Cor 4:8–9).

This describes the precarious character of his life and work, but then he goes on to heighten the paradox, and again we find our apostolic experience enshrined in the statement:

> . . . always carrying in the body the death of Jesus, so that the life of Jesus may also be manifested in our bodies. For while we live we are always being given up to death for Jesus' sake, so that the life of Jesus may be manifested in our mortal flesh. So death is at work in us, but life in you (2 Cor 4:10–12).

Death is at work in us, but life in you. The suffering and death of Jesus is not a once-and-for-all event touching only him. It is something all of us participate in over and over in many ways, without its necessarily ever coming to the drama of an actual crucifixion. The mystery at work here, as in the case of Jesus himself, is that the death we die is somehow life-giving for others. It is fruitful, even while it seems to be destroying us. In the midst of our suffering and inadequacy, we mediate something to others that is not our own possession and which we usually cannot even feel passing through our system. We instinctively suppose we should work from strength, handing on to others the riches that are ours. Instead, we often do our best work when we operate from weakness and totally empty hands, passing on something we do not possess, producing effects we can in no way explain out of who or how we are. God's economy is bizarre; there is no employment quite as baffling as his. Again Paul speaks of it:

> When I came to you, brothers and sisters, I did not come proclaiming to you the testimony of God in lofty words or wisdom. For I decided to know nothing among you except Jesus Christ and him crucified. And I was with you in weakness and in much fear and trembling; and my speech and my message were not in plausible words of wisdom, but in demonstration of the Spirit and of power, that your faith might not rest in the wisdom of human beings but in the power of God (1 Cor 2:1–5).

There is good reason for dwelling this way on our involvement in the paschal mystery even when we are trying to help. For unless we understand it, we will shrink back from agreeing to serve others in a helping capacity, precisely because we so keenly feel weakness, fear and trembling, thorns in the flesh, death in our own mouths. Common sense dictates staying out of other people's lives. But God's is not exactly a common sense economy. The fact is that some of our best preachers have to drag themselves into the pulpit to do it, some of our best consolers dread nothing more than having to go out and be with those who mourn, some of our best prayer leaders pray with heavy hearts, and some of our best counselors and therapists have little sense most of the time that they are doing anything for those who sit before them. They achieve what they achieve because it is not really their achieving. What is asked of them is simply that they be willing, in faith, to present themselves, to go there, to open their mouths and speak what comes out. It would take a lifetime to get ready, and then we wouldn't be ready. Jeremiah said, "Ah, Lord God! Behold, I do not know how to speak, for I am only a youth." But God said to him:

> Do not say, "I am only a youth"; for to all to whom I send you you shall go, and whatever I command you you shall

speak. Be not afraid of them, for I am with you to deliver
you, says the Lord (Jer 1:6–8).

Moses humbly offered the same demurrer, and got the same reply
(Ex 3). Paul felt it too, as we have seen, but after the Lord's word
to him, he had a kind of conversion experience, acquiesced in the
mystery of God's ways, and ended by saying:

> I will all the more gladly boast of my weaknesses, that the
> power of Christ may rest upon me. For the sake of Christ,
> then, I am content with weaknesses, insults, hardships, per-
> secutions, and calamities; for when I am weak, then I am
> strong (2 Cor 12:9–10).

The helper is sacrament for the other. Like all sacraments we
are inadequate to the reality we flesh forth. We are mere earthen vessels, to show that the amazing power belongs to God and not to us
(2 Cor 4:7).

QUESTIONS FOR REFLECTION AND DISCUSSION

1. What does sacrament mean to you?

2. How are Christ, the church, and the Christian helper sacramental?

3. Where else do you see sacramentality in your world of experience?

4. What sense does it make for one limited human being to pose
   as helper to another where the lofty ideals of the Christian life
   are concerned?

SUGGESTIONS FOR FURTHER READING

E. Schillebeeckx   *Christ the Sacrament of the Encounter With
                        God*

Henri Nouwen	*Wounded Healer*
Vatican II	*Dogmatic Constitution on the Church,* especially Chapters I & II.
Avery Dulles	*Models of the Church*

2. Establishing an Orientation

In the last chapter we looked at the helping relationship in the context of Christian faith. Now let us focus on the role of the helper and try to come to a more exact notion of what he or she is trying to do. A relationship can come to grief if we do not understand what we are doing. We ourselves can come to grief if we ask the impossible of ourselves. So let us attempt a role description, first setting forth what the helping role is, then clarifying it further by stating what it is not.

WHAT IT IS ...

1. To listen

A helper is, in the first instance, one who agrees to listen. Anything else that may happen in the relationship will derive from this. Listening to another may not seem like much, but its effect happens to be very therapeutic. Everyone yearns to be heard. But so many cannot find anyone who will listen, or do not trust most people to be able to handle what they really need to say. So they come to you.

Listening is not always easy. It takes time, and the time might be inconvenient besides. It demands really being for the other during that period, fully present and attentive, one's own needs and concerns set aside. This is exacting. Listening might mean being afflicted with the most profound sense of helplessness, having the springs of sorrow touched, seeing one's dearest convictions called painfully into question by the experience and testimony of another. The person may not be attractive, might be telling a dull and too oft repeated tale, might be making mountains out of molehills, might be demanding and even manipulative. These are the hazards. Nevertheless there comes to me a human being whom God created and loves. There comes a sister or brother for whom Christ died (Rm 14:15). There enters a suffering fellow pilgrim. The first thing one consents to do is to welcome and listen. It is an act of love.

2. To Be a Companion

The willingness to enter into a helping relationship is essentially the willingness to be a companion—not a teacher, not a savior, but a companion. One agrees to go along. The word "companion" means one who breaks bread with another. People who break bread together share life. It might be nice to be able to do more for someone else—to be savior, wonder-worker, supplier of every need. The helper cannot promise so much, but one gift he or she can give, and that is to be a companion. I will go with you on your journey, take to heart all that concerns you, be there when you need me. This is companionship.

It is a limited role to be sure. But if it does nothing else it lifts the dread burden of loneliness from the shoulders of the other, and that makes all other burdens lighter. Camus' brief statement is an accurate utterance of the hope of one who opens his or her life to another.

Do not walk behind me. I may not lead.
Do not walk in front of me. I may not follow.
Just walk beside me, and be my friend.

The helper does not always solve the problem or take the pain away. But he or she is friend and resource, to explore with another, to watch another with concern, to listen and respond, to be available.

3. To Love

To listen attentively to another and to go with another in companionship are expressions of love. To do either without love is an empty gesture and bears no fruit. The helper loves the other. Now there is no greater thing we can do for another human being than to love him or her. We touch here a truth just large enough to be easily overlooked. I am supposed to be a Christian helper, so I snap to attention. I put on a hat. I will be a sterling model of the Christian life, a shrewd analyst, an expert advisor. I will also develop a pep talk. These things have their place, but to put them first is to mistake the lesser for the greater. The most helpful thing one human being can do for another is to love him or her, and this is as valid for helping relationships as for any other kind.

Karl Menninger, after decades of work in psychotherapy, lays aside all learned talk both of psychic maladies and of therapeutic techniques, and utters one simple overarching truth: It is unlove that makes people unwell, and it is love and love alone that can make them well again. His contention is buttressed by more general studies and surveys, in which it has been shown that those therapists are most successful in bringing health back to their clients who are best able to convey love. Their theoretical framework may be Freudian, Jungian, Rogerian, Gestalt, Transactional Analysis, or anything else; the most telling factor is still the ability to communicate care, reverence, and hope to the troubled person. This explains in part why some psychotherapists seem to do so little for people even after months and years of appointments, and some complete amateurs are able to make a significant difference in a short time. In my own years of receiving spiritual direction from various directors, it is clear to me that those who helped me the most were not the eldest of them, the holiest, or the best schooled in counseling and spiritual direction; it was those who loved me the most. How did it work? They enabled me to believe in myself, to rejoice in my own being and gifts, to accept the mystery of my life in hope, and to make the most of it. Compared to this, analysis, advice, summaries of treatises, and exhortations to the heights come to very little.

Consider the effectiveness of Jesus, that great healer of the human spirit. He was not a trained therapist, nor even a trained priest or rabbi. He worked transformations in the lives of people because he loved them. He gave Magdalen a new lease on life because he loved her (Lk 7). He enabled Peter to become a fisher of human beings because he loved him in spite of himself (Lk 5). He got Zaccheus to come down from his tree and give half his goods to the poor becaused he loved him (Lk 19). And he heals each of us in exactly the same way, accepting us in spite of our sinfulness, staying with us in spite of our waywardness, loving us in spite of everything that is wrong with us. This is what keeps the sun coming up in the morning. Love is creative and transformative power, coming into our lives always as the great surprise, filling our sails with a fresh breeze.

> And Jesus stopped and said, "Call him." And they called the blind man, saying to him, "Take heart; rise, he is calling you." And throwing off his mantle he sprang up and came to Jesus" (Mk 10:49–50).

How does one person love another? Love is partly a gift, partly a choice. One dimension of the experience of loving someone is gift: to me it is given deeply to understand and appreciate this person, and to care for him or her. Some individuals seem to have the capacity to love many people, and to love them easily. This is the first thing to look at when considering one's suitability for being a Christian helper. Am I the sort of person who genuinely likes people, who readily sees the good in them, who postively enjoys getting to know them? If so, then I have one of the basic gifts of the Christian helper.

Love is also partly a choice. It is the choice to respect another, to recognize his or her autonomy, to presume good will. It is the choice to welcome another warmly, and to provide an environment in which the other can feel safe. It is the choice to listen to another with attention and interest, to affirm and confirm all that one can, to share something of one's own experience, and to apologize when one offends. "Love is patient and kind," Paul says. "Love bears all things, believes all things, hopes all things, endures all things" (1 Cor 13:4–7). These are the choice aspects of love. The more one likes and feels enthusiasm for the person who comes, the easier it is to do these things. But even in the absence of such feelings, one can choose to do the deeds of love.

4. To Be Oneself

The helper is one who is willing to be him- or herself. Not a professional hiding behind a mask, but a fellow struggler of flesh and blood, with his or her own burdens, doubts, fears, weaknesses, temptations, guilt. To be oneself in a helping conversation might be to allow oneself to cry with one in deep sorrow, to express outrage as one listens to a person suffering injustice, to admit that one is just as baffled by the mystery of life and of God as one's puzzled friend. These are not studied or affected responses, given because calculated to be helpful, but the natural responses of heart and mind as one enters freely into the experience of another. To be oneself is the key, expressing puzzlement if puzzlement is felt, affirmation if affirmation is felt, disagreement if disagreement is felt—but all of these modestly, as having no more authority than that of one's personal reactions.

Presuming normal personal development, common sense, and a reasonable freedom from bias, simply to be oneself and to react naturally to what one hears is to be a reality principle in the life of the other. Everything that has been said so far about the role of the helper boils down to taking a genuine interest in and caring for the person. Now we are talking about what contributes to changing the person's perspective on reality. Each of us is limited in our perspectives on our own affairs. Each of us is a poor judge in our own case. To hear another agree and confirm, or simply understand and accept without condemning, or remind us of some obvious aspects of a situation we have overlooked in our preoccupation with other aspects, or tell us rather obvious things about ourselves that we have forgotten—these are very helpful contributions to our self-understanding and our perceptions. We get down on ourselves, and another person speaks of our goodness and our gifts, which strike him or her as so much larger. We describe apparently insoluble dilemmas, and another person suggests possible courses of action we had never considered. We confess our hidden doubts and fears as problems uniquely our own, and another person makes us feel at home in the human race. We describe the world as constituted in a certain way, and another person says he or she sees it differently. We keep wrestling with and rearranging the superficial factors in a situation, and another person leads us to a deeper consideration and engagement of it. The helper in all these situations is doing nothing more complicated than being him- or herself, reacting naturally as a person's narrative unfolds, asking the questions, making the observations, sharing the feelings that occur. Thus the helper functions as a kind of reality principle, sometimes confirming, sometimes challenging the other to view things in a different light.

WHAT IT IS NOT ...

We can further clarify the helper's role if we look at some of the things it is not.

1. To Be Responsible for Another Person's Life

The helper does not take responsibility for the life of the other. To take that responsibility is first of all to assume a heavy burden, and a charge ultimately impossible to execute. Further it does a grave injustice to the person seeking help, since it keeps him or her in a position of dependency and immaturity. The temptation here is a subtle one, whose source may lie on either side of the relationship. The person seeking help may want to get rid of responsibility; the person offering help may positively relish dependents and authority. But this displacement is an unconscionable violation of mature personhood.

To the average person called upon to help another, as well as to the balanced person seeking help, the statement of this principle is an immense relief. Each, for good reasons, would avoid a relationship defined in dependency terms. But a relationship defined in mutually free and responsible terms is palatable. A qualification should be put in before we leave this point. This refusal to assume responsibility for another's life or to foster dependency does not mean we will let no one cry on our shoulder, come back a second time, ask for advice, or seek more companionship for a period than would be usual. There is a certain element of dependency in the very seeking of help. The point is that the ultimate objective will always be to give people's lives back to them, to help them make their own decisions and be responsible for them, to increase their sense of a healthy autonomy.

2. To Remove Problem and Pain

Another presumption that defeats helping relationships from the start is the helper's presumption that he or she is being asked to solve the problem or put an end to the suffering. This is usually impossible, and is rarely being asked for. But if the helper assumes that this is the assignment, there is bound to be anxiety, frustration, and a strong urge to flee all such situations. If, for example, someone is grieving over the loss of a spouse, there is no way the death can be undone or the pain taken away. If someone is dying of cancer, no conversation is going to avert death or abolish anguish. If a teenager is having trouble living in a home racked with marital conflict, he or she will most likely still be living there and trying to cope with the situation when the conversation is over. We do what we can to ameliorate problems and assuage sorrows. But there are a lot of human problems which cannot be solved, a lot of suffering that cannot be taken away. Usually when someone comes to us with a grief or a problem, he or she does not expect us to be able to change a situation very much if at all. It is something else they seek. Keeping that in mind makes the task a great deal easier to bear.

3. To Offer Greater Experience, Wisdom, and Holiness

Some misgivings besetting the helper stem from the presumption that one must be older, wiser, and holier than the person seeking help. All of these things might be considerable assets, but they are not strictly necessary. The great advantage the helper has is that he or she is distinct from the person seeking help, and so is not involved in the same way. A young spiritual director can often spot the self-deceptions of an older person, simply because they are quite obvious—except to the person suffering them. The director has self-deceptions too. We are all too close to ourselves, and vitally depend on the corrective supplied by an outsider's perspective. As with holiness, so with age and wisdom. One might have them in lesser measure than the one seeking help, and still be very useful just by reason of greater objectivity and ordinary insight.

The helper need not have had exactly the experience the other person is talking about. One can minister very effectively to the dying without having died oneself. One can be of assistance to the married without being married oneself. One can understand and help the homosexual without being gay oneself. Again here, having had the experience would usually be a great advantage—if one has the good sense to realize that the other's experience may not be precisely the same. But one need not have trod exactly the same winepress, because there are analogies in experience, and we can understand the other person's situation from experiences of our own which bear it some resemblance. One may not be a chronic depressive, and yet understand depression quite well from a personal brush with it. One may not be married, yet deal well with marital problems on the basis of having grown up in a family, having married friends, knowing the experience of friendship, and understanding something of male and female psychology. Thus, some priests have been fine marriage counselors. And a Roman Catholic sister who left her community told me that the person who understood her best was an older married man of a different race and a different faith. Empathy is the key, and some people have it in extraordinary measure.

There are times when we do *not* understand, and cannot enter the experience of another. These are not times to say, "I know just what you mean." They are rather times to say, "I've never had that experience myself. I wish I could understand it better." And sometimes we are asked questions to which the only truthful answer is: "That's something I guess I've never really thought about." Nothing is quite so refreshing as honesty, and it pays dividends in the long run, deepening the bond of trust. It gives the person the assurance that you will say what you really think, that you are not afraid, when the time is right, to say those three difficult words: "I don't know." Such an admission will usually not bring the conversation to a standstill. It may give it a push, inviting the other to elaborate and clarify what is not yet clear even to him- or herself. The helper will probably be brought to deeper insight too, or at least to further reflection.

4. To Make the Other a Different Person

It is salutary to face the limits of how much growth one may be able to occasion in the life of another. The other has a long history, a physical and psychic facticity, an ambience of impinging influences. It might be clear to us that what another person needs most is to fall in love. But it is difficult to make that happen. There are some marriages we would love to be able to save, and will not be able to. The alcoholic needs to stop drinking, the scrupulous person needs to put aside irrational anxieties, someone else needs to grow up. But we cannot make these things happen. We may be directing someone's annual retreat, and, after listening to the person a few times, know clearly what grace he or she needs. But we cannot produce it, and may have miscalculated its opportuneness anyway. Human beings grow organically, and the operative factors in their growth are multiple, some environmental and some constitutional, all evasive of management. The helper is but one of those factors, and has only a modest function. One may be able to plant a seed in someone's mind that will bear fruit later. One may be able to help set up an occasion or situation which could foster the needed growth. But there are countless factors outside the helper's control, including the freedom of the person who comes. So the limits are sharply set. This can be very frustrating, but will be less so if one approaches helping relationships with realistic rather than unrealistic expectations. The butterfly cannot be made to emerge from the cocoon before it is time. And beagles are beagles. Here it is instructive to remember Paul's reflections on his work with other Christians:

> What then is Apollos? What is Paul? Servants through whom you believed, as the Lord assigned to each. I planted, Apollos watered, but God gave the growth. So neither the person who plants nor the person who waters is anything, but only God who gives the growth (1 Cor 3:5-7).

There is one important thing to remember when one is feeling inadequate to the challenge of a particular helping relationship, whether the root of the diffidence be apparently inferior qualifications, or an especially tough case. In most circumstances, the persons who came to you chose you. They did it for reasons which make sense at least to them. Just as they need help precisely because it is difficult for them to grasp their own situation, you might be suffering from the same lack of insight when you decide you cannot help them. One principle which may prove liberating in such situations, especially for those who tend to disparage themselves, is: If they are crazy enough to ask me, I'm crazy enough to say yes.

QUESTIONS FOR REFLECTION AND DISCUSSION

1. What is the role of the Christian helper? What are some common ways of misunderstanding it?

2. Why would you or would you not agree, if asked by the person, to be a Christian helper to:
   a. a homosexual if you are heterosexual
   b. an ordained person
   c. a Christian of another denomination
   d. a nun some twenty years older than yourself
   e. a close friend
   f. a lay-person if you are a religious, or vice versa.

3. Why do some people hate to hear other people talk about their problems? What is your own position on this?

4. Why do some people like nothing better than to give other people advice? What is your own position on this?

5. If you have ever had the experience of being helped by another Christian in the manner we are describing, what things did that person do with you that you would imitate with others, and what things that you would avoid?

SUGGESTIONS FOR FURTHER READING

Karl Menninger	*The Vital Balance*
Carl Rogers	*Client-Centered Therapy*
Eugene Kennedy	*On Becoming a Counselor*
Paul Tournier	*The Meaning of Persons*

3. Counseling and Spiritual Direction

What is the difference between counseling and spiritual direction? And how might they be intertwined in the actual practice of the one or the other? These are questions of importance especially to the spiritual director. "It seems that all I'm doing is counseling," a director might say in dismay. "Do I have to be a psychotherapist to be a good spiritual director?" another will ask. And another, "Is it wise to try to be spiritual director to somebody who is in psychotherapy?" The matter is further complicated when the Christian psychologist interposes, "I find myself doing quite a bit of what I would call spiritual direction." These issues are not so easy to sort out.

In this chapter we change our terminology somewhat. We have been speaking so far of Christian helpers, and conceiving that function broadly enough to include all sorts of relationships. Here the focus is somewhat tighter, and the classical term "spiritual director" is employed. This designation has its difficulties. The term "spiritual" suggests too strict a confinement of the interest, as we shall see. The term "director" is too imperative for the kind of relating we have already espoused. In spite of its shortcomings the designation remains current, however, and we will use it in this chapter to denote a contract in which the person seeking help is interested in regular conversations oriented quite specifically to spiritual growth. What then is the relationship between psychological counseling and spiritual direction?

One way the relationship is commonly misread is to see spiritual direction as concerned with a special area of life in which counseling has little interest—one's relationship with God. Psychological counselors are understood to deal with personality problems—neuroses, psychoses, hang-ups, anxieties, depressions. You go to them to get fixed. Spiritual directors, on the other hand, deal not so much with problems as with progress, progress in the spiritual life. You talk with them about specialized human experiences—prayer, religious vocation, temptations, delusions, apostolic interests. Their preparation consists not in mastering theories of personality, but in mastering John of the Cross, Teresa of Avila, Ignatius Loyola, and other authorities in the field of spiritual development, who can chart the ordinary course of growth in prayer, the signs of a vocation, and patterns of subtle temptation for people seriously pursuing God in their lives. On this reading, these two sorts of helping relationships have quite different concerns.

Such a view is inadequate to both members of the supposed antithesis. It views psychological counseling in too problem-centered a way, when in our day psychotherapy is often sought not for problem-solving but for life-enhancement. The client desires deeper self-knowledge and a finer integration. Furthermore, some schools of psychotherapy regard a person's relationship with God as a crucial factor in psychic wholeness. Where spiritual direction is concerned, this interpretation labors under a very narrow theology of God's presence and activity. Let us explore this matter further.

God of Nature and History

Religion is not a distinct area of life, but a dimension of all life. God is not present to us only when we pray, nor is spiritual growth confined to such times. He is present always, the relationship to him is constant, and growth is possible anytime. There is no area of human life in which God is uninterested, no corner of it to which he is not present, and therefore no aspect of life which would be foreign or inappropriate matter in a conversation with a spiritual director. The key to understanding here is to scrap the model of areas of life, or distinct realms—work, play, social life, prayer, sleep—and to substitute for it a model of levels or dimensions of experience. God is the deepest dimension of all experience. The vision is well expressed by St. Paul in his speech in the Areopagus of Athens:

> And he made ... human beings ... that they should seek God, in the hope that they might feel after him and find him. Yet he is not far from each one of us, for "In him we live and move and have our being," as even some of your poets have said (Acts 17:26–28).

If in God we live and move and have our being, he is present at least at the edges of consciousness always, in the background, in the depths. Our relationship with him, then, is not a special activity, but a constant reality; not an occasional telephone call, but a long sit together.

Contemporary theology is unanimous in accenting the presence of the divine within the ordinary human. Without denigrating the special activities of prayer or sacramental celebration, it stresses that the ordinary locus of the encounter with God is our daily round of social relationships and solitude, work and play, joys, sorrows, and hopes. We do not have to go apart to seek God, but will find him in the commonplace if we are sensitive to his ways of showing his glory, giving his gifts, moving us to the good, occasioning our growth. On this view there is nothing profane, nothing merely secular, nothing purely "natural." Reality is suffused with the presence of God. And grace is not a mysterious quantity flowing through the channels of prayer and sacraments, but the gracious ambience in which all life is lived because God loves us, discloses himself to us, and draws us to himself always. Gerard Manley Hopkins puts it this way:

> The world is charged with the grandeur of God.
> It will flame out, like shining from shook foil;
> It gathers to a greatness, like the ooze of oil
> Crushed. Why do men then now not reck his rod?

And e. e. cummings:

> i thank you God for most this amazing
> day: for the leaping greenly spirits of trees
> and a blue true dream of sky; and for everything
> which is natural which is infinite which is yes . . .
>
> (now the ears of my ears awake and
> now the eyes of my eyes are opened)

This contemporary view, which puts the spiritual life on rather different bases than it has sometimes been, has excellent biblical foundations. For in the Bible, the world is God's creation and self-manifestation.

> O Lord, how manifold are your works!
> In wisdom you have made them all;
> the earth is full of your creatures.
> Yonder is the sea, great and wide,
> which teems with things innumerable,
> living things both small and great (Ps 104).

> The heavens are telling the glory of God;
> and the firmament proclaims his handiwork.
> Day to day pours forth speech,
> and night to night declares knowledge (Ps 19).

> O come, let us worship and bow down,
> let us kneel before the Lord, our Maker!
> For he is our God, and we are the people of his pasture,
> and the sheep of his hand (Ps 95).

In the cities, we can be out of touch with nature, and so lose some of that sense of mystery which people living closer to nature had and have. Perhaps for city-dwellers, more than for these folks, other persons will be the principal manifestation of the mystery and glory of God. But urbanites have a richness of experience to recover by walking in parks or woods once in a while, going to zoos and arboretums, and spending time at rivers, lakes, and oceans. All of this is the plane of nature, God's ongoing creation and self-revelation.

The other plane of his presence is history, or the dynamic of events. The Hebrews came to know him in historical events before they grew sensitive to his presence and majesty in nature. In the things which happened to them, they perceived a benevolent guiding hand. What had seemed mere chance or the result of good human planning took on increasingly the hue of a particular providence. Their primal experience of God was that he was savior and deliverer in the events of their lives. They found him to be not distant and disinterested, but concerned, resourceful, and faithful. The Old Testament is mainly a book of memories, memories of God's presence and actions on behalf of his people, recollections of his promise to be covenanted with them always. Its usefulness for us lies not in its cataloging of past events, but in its alerting us to be on the watch for God's activity in our own lives. For surely the God who manifested his presence so forcibly in events long past has not grown silent and aloof since, leaving us the anomaly of a brief historical moment of hyperactivity on a very long band of human history. The Old Testament period is more congruously viewed as the paradigmatic revelation of the fact and pattern of God's presence to all history.

God the Horizon, God the Depth

Two contemporary theologians, among others, have offered illuminating metaphors for heightening one's awareness of God's presence in life. Paul Tillich speaks of God as "the depth" in things. To people who say they know no God, he suggests that they call to mind their experiences of depth, wherever they occur—in beauty, in love, in terror, in wonder, in loneliness, in contingency, in peace. The experience of depth, he maintains, is the experience of God, for God is the depth-dimension of all reality. This metaphoric description of the mystery of God is helpful in sensitizing us to ways we often meet him without realizing it.

So does Karl Rahner's metaphor of God as the horizon of all

experience. A horizon is the backdrop of the things we see, itself never directly seen, but the background against which we see everything else. God is the horizon into which all our questing presses, for our questing never rests at any object it attains. God is the background into which all our questioning probes, since every answer we receive only prompts a new question as we push relentlessly into the mystery of reality. All our experiences of the good and the true stand revealed in their limitedness and unsatisfactoriness against the backdrop of the mystery of God, partly disclosed in them and ever abiding as a lure beyond them. With this vague experience of God at the edges of consciousness most of us can identify, and Rahner's metaphor, like Tillich's, goads us to greater awareness. Both ground a contemplative vision of life, and offer broad bases for a spirituality.

This whole idea of creation and history as the language of God's self-expression is well illustrated in the experience of Helen Keller, the woman born blind and deaf. With these two primary avenues of human learning closed to her, the little girl Helen scarcely understood the world at all. Her environment, so sharply confined, was all a meaningless concreteness of tactile sensations, odors, and tastes. Then a teacher came into the life of the child and labored to impart the notion of symbolic communication. She took Helen's hand and, by movements of her own hand, spelled out into it the names of objects in a devised alphabetic language. At first Helen did not get the message; the movements of her teacher's hand in hers were just like all other tactile pushes, pulls, and pressures, having no reference to anything beyond themselves. Then one dramatic day the teacher's long and patient struggle paid off, and Helen got the message that Anne's repeated frantic movements *meant* the water which she was simultaneously pouring over her hands. Helen then first grasped the notion of language, or symbolic communication. She understood that a sight or a sound or a touch can point beyond itself to something else, to which it serves as expression. That was the day huge doors swung open for Helen, her horizons of experience immensely enlarged.

In exactly the same way, faith opens the eyes and ears of human understanding, so that we no longer stop at the mere appearances of things, but see through them to their depths. For the person of faith, the world is transparency, pointing beyond itself. All ordinary experience is symbolic communication from a mysterious source. Things are not just things and events just events, on the plane of the physical movements in Helen Keller's hand. They point beyond themselves to the God who speaks them as his self-expression and self-disclosure. Thus the word which became flesh in Jesus of Nazareth was already being spoken in nature and history from the beginning, and it continues to be spoken in nature and history, because the word is as old as God himself, and all that was made was made through the word (Jn 1:1–3). When Jesus heals the blind man in John's gospel, the real opening of the eyes takes place not when the man sees his parents and neighbors for the first time, but when he perceives in the flesh of Nazareth the Son of God, and worships him (Jn 9:38). It is faith that opens our eyes to the reality in which we live.

Awareness and Response

All of this has been considered to make it clear that spiritual direction has to do with more than a special interest area of life, a separate experience or set of activities for which some people have a taste, others not. God is the deepest dimension in all the areas of human life, and thus all areas are open to spiritual direction. The purpose of direction will be to sensitize people further to the presence and action of God in their lives, and to assist them to make a fuller and more appropriate response to it. The objectives are that simple: awareness, response. The spiritual director is as interested as the psychological counselor in a person's living situation, his or her work, social relationships, recreation, self-image, conflicts, and sufferings. But unlike the ordinary psychological counselor, the spiritual director will be finally interested in the ultimate dimension of all this experience, namely: Where is God in all this? Where in your life do you encounter him most powerfully? What do you think he is moving or calling you to? How would he want you to grow spiritually through the routine of your work, the conflicts and joys of your living situation, the important relationships of your life, your temptations, your feelings about yourself? How might faith, hope, and love pervade your ordinary perceptions and choices more completely? The concern of spiritual direction is not a separate realm, but the deepest dimension of every realm. It is content to spend time with people over this or that situation, this or that personal growth need, without undue reliance on God-talk. Some people require particular attention at the level of their self-image, in the working out of a particular relationship, in the discovery of their gifts. This is the important work, since human beings are one in their life, though divisible conceptually into physical, emotional, intellectual, and spiritual components. The whole person has to come along in growth, and work at any level is germane to the building of God's temple. What endows the spiritual-direction relationship with its peculiar stamp is that the context of the whole endeavor is faith, and that its ultimate concern is awareness of and response to God in one's life.

Besides this difference in orientation, the spiritual director will often use a tactic the psychological counselor does not employ. He or she will send the person to prayer about the matter in question. Particular scripture passages appropriate to the situation might even be suggested. The objective is to put the person in closer contact with the influence of God. In psychological counseling, two persons talk things through. In spiritual direction, two persons talk things through too, but both try to be maximally aware of another voice also—the leadings of the Lord in the situation.

Out of this concern spring questions the spiritual director might legitimately put to the psychological counselor who shows no interest in this ultimate dimension. How can he or she conceive of real psychic health without any advertence to God? The product of psychotherapy is human wholeness. But can there be human wholeness where there is no attunement to the final source of human meaning? What sense can people make of life without any faith, any hope, any charity? How do they cope with suffering, with death, with guilt? How do they live with that abiding human dissatisfaction which is the cue that our final destiny transcends the limits of time? Perhaps people can come to some kind of stoic settlement with life strictly on its own terms. But one wonders whether this sort of bleak resignation can be called a real healing of the human spirit.

By the same token the spiritual director does well to appreciate the concerns of the psychological counselor. Does the director advert sufficiently to the psychological bases of human spiritual growth?

More prayer is not always the best answer to inner conflict, nor is greater Christian forbearance always the answer to interpersonal stress or oppressive social situations. Frequent confession of sins might fail to reach the root of recurrent difficulties. And the cultivation of an attitude of humility in the name of spiritual progress might stand in the way of personal maturation and the assumption of responsibility for one's life. It does not take much acquaintance with the spiritual formation of times past to discover that things like religious obedience, humility, charity, fidelity, delicacy of conscience, zeal for perfection, and thirst for souls can all go awry, and work against rather than for one's own and others' genuine well-being.

Ideally, then, the Christian helper seeks a harmony of the best that psychological and spiritual insights have to offer. It is peaceful, free, and happy human beings we wish to bring to the fullness of their possibilities. The director need not be a trained clinical psychologist. His or her expertise lies in a different area. What is important is that he or she be a reasonably integrated person, possess a knowledge of ordinary human psychodynamics, and have a genuine reverence for all the dimensions of human personhood. It is vital that his or her spirituality be comprehensive, careful not to set God against the world, or the "will of God" against normal human self-realization and fulfillment. God is one, and he is a God of life.

Good psychotherapy works to help people cope with reality, to live in it peaceably and to deal with it constructively. Spiritual direction could hardly do better. Reality is God's creation, and history is in his hands. Coping well with reality is coping well with God. Escaping reality into a separate realm, however spiritual the motive, runs the risk of missing the real encounter with God and the kinds of growth that come from that encounter.

With this, we should have answers to the questions which opened the chapter. A spiritual director does a certain amount of ordinary psychological counseling, but with a particular finality. A psychological counselor might share that finality, and do some spiritual direction incidental to his or her main work. Where a psychotherapist does not share such a concern, a spiritual director might work simultaneously with someone in therapy on that person's spiritual growth. More will be said on this last point in a later chapter.

QUESTIONS FOR REFLECTION AND DISCUSSION

1. How do you experience God in your life? Are the categories of biblical thought any help to you in recognizing these experiences? Are the metaphors of Tillich and Rahner?

2. How would you deal with someone who told you he or she has no experience of God, either in prayer or anywhere else?

3. What is the objective of the spiritual direction or Christian-helping relationship?

4. How much of a counselor ought a spiritual director to be?

5. Of what importance for growth in the spiritual life are such things as the way one feels about oneself, one's success or failure in relating to others, one's recreation or the lack of it?

6. What danger, if any, do you see in spiritual-direction sessions which concern themselves only with prayer, the sacraments, vocation, temptations, spiritual reading?

7. What are the basic interpersonal gifts or skills common to successful counseling and spiritual direction?

SUGGESTIONS FOR FURTHER READING

Gregory Baum   *Man Becoming*

Karl Rahner   *Do You Believe in God?*

Paul Tillich   *The Dynamics of Faith*

John L. McKenzie   *Theology of the Old Testament*

4. Growth in the Christian Life

A helping relationship in the context of Christian faith is aimed at growth in the Christian life. The question is, what is this growth? Can we be more concrete about our goal? Such definition is crucial to the whole helping enterprise. It is very hard to get to Xanadu if you don't know where Xanadu is.

A lot of ink has been spilled on the question of Christian spirituality, It goes in many directions, but all the radii fan out from a common center, Jesus Christ. Paul names him the new Adam (Rm 5:12–21, 1 Cor 15:42–50), which means he is the second and greater progenitor of the human race. The first three gospels call him the beloved Son in whom the Father is well pleased (Mk 1:11, 9:7, and parallels), and admonish us to listen to him. John sees him as the Word of God in the flesh (Jn 1:1–18), which means God's whole message to us about life is visible in him. In the same gospel, Jesus is portrayed as saying of himself: "I am the Way and the Truth and the Life" (Jn 14:6). The answer to the question about growth in the Christian life is then a person, Jesus Christ. We reach the fullness of our human potential as God envisages that potential, in the measure that we are conformed to Jesus. Let us examine, at least briefly, what seems to be at the heart of his way of life and his teaching.

His Life

The strongest feature of the life of Jesus of Nazareth is that he lives it with God. He speaks of his Father continually, showing an habitual awareness of him in the way he perceives reality and responds to it. One thing he wants above all: to do always the things that please the Father (Jn 8:29), to accomplish his will (Jn 4:34). He is seen regularly at prayer, strengthening the vital bond, sensitizing himself to the Father's leadings in his life. His impact on others produces in them an impression to which they testify in chorus, the gospels being their testimony: In this man we have met God in a degree that puts Jesus in a class by himself. Jesus, summing up his life in a prayer on the eve of his passion, says: "I have glorified you on earth, having accomplished the work which you gave me to do" (Jn 17:4).

What is surprising is not so much his orientation, but the manner in which he lives it out. It is steeped in ordinariness. He does not leave the crowd to go off and live a more ascetic life, nor does he persuade his followers to do so. He does not lay stress on fasting or other ascetic practices, or present celibacy as the distinctive feature of his way of life. On the contrary, he is seen at table in questionable company with sufficient frequency to earn the name of glutton and drunkard, friend to tax collectors and sinners (Lk 7:34). And though he is celibate, his chosen followers, the Twelve are, with the possible exception of John, all married men. Jesus does take time to pray regularly. But the typical situation in which he is found in the gospels is a social setting of one kind or another. The usual thing he is doing is helping people in some way—now healing, now reconciling, now feeding, now teaching them. He is not a priest, scribe, or pharisee. He takes his stance outside the religious institution of his day, a layman without connections or authorization. But his life is ministry, his milieu all human society.

His Teaching

What does he teach? He teaches exactly what he lives. For one thing, he teaches a contemplative vision of life. All the vehicle of his instruction is the ordinary stuff of this world, seen through to its significance in God. He calls attention to the word of God spoken in the change of seasons, the growth of seeds, the birth of a child, the harbingers of weather change, the storm at sea, the dinner party, the judge, the ruler, the rich man and the beggar, the steward, the householder, the child. He finds lessons of eternal significance in these and many similar earthly realities. He is much more than a skilled pedagogue adapting to the thought-world of his audience. He is a first-rate religious teacher because he is a profound contemplative.

In his teaching he stresses certain things. He attaches great importance to simplicity of life, not laying up treasure on earth, yet not being anxious about the means of life (Mt 6:19–34). His parable of the rich man and poor Lazarus instructs us to share what we have with those in need (Lk 16:19–31). His parable of the good samaritan makes it both goods and services (Lk 10:25–37). He urges forgiveness and reconciliation, not judging, loving even enemies (Lk 6:32–38). He keeps people reminded of the shortness of life, the preciousness of the present day, the need to stay awake (Mk 13:32–37). With regard to God, he teaches trust in all circumstances, hope in the unexpected deliverance, confidence in God's forgiveness and the constancy of his love for all of his children. He stresses the importance of listening to the truth wherever it is spoken, and of speaking the truth whether it is profitable or not. Where suffering is concerned, he teaches a mystery: that suffering and dying are not the last word, but passage to new life. He does not say much in explanation of it, but he teaches that our God is a God at work in the depth and darkness of things, somehow bringing life out of death, good out of evil, meaning out of meaninglessness.

Now if we look back over these teachings, we can see that there is nothing arcane or esoteric about them. They are plain truths, intended not for a select few but for everyone, livable in *all* circumstances and styles of life. He shares them not just with the Twelve, but with the multitudes.

The religious genius of Jesus is to radicalize and to simplify, to get at the root of our relationship with God and to sum it up in a few words. And so, in the last days of his ministry, when a scribe asks him what is the greatest commandment, he pulls his whole teaching and entire way of life together into a single summary rule of life:

> You shall love the Lord your God with all your heart, and with all your soul, and with all your mind, and with all your strength . . . You shall love your neighbor as yourself (Mk 12:29–31).

No one will say this program is easy, but it is certainly not complicated. It demands absolutely everything of us, all day every day, but the content of the demand is basic and clear.

It is as if Jesus surveyed the religious scene of his day and said to himself: These are good people, but they are all confused. They think God wants religious services, tithes, and the strict observance of law. In fact, he wants their hearts. They think he wants religiosity, complete with sackcloth and a daily regimen. He would much rather see them love one another and share what they have with one another, so that everybody has life. They think he wants them to reject the world and isolate themselves from it, when in fact he wants them to enjoy it and give thanks for it, and to work to make it more human. They think he wants them to live in fear, fear of going wrong and fear of him, when in fact he wants them to live in joy and freedom. They think he wants them to walk about with their heads down because of all their failures, when in fact he wants them to trust like children in his forgiveness and the dependability of his love. They think they have to earn their way with him and win a reward if they can, when in fact he wants them to accept his acceptance of them as a gift quite undeserved.

And so we find this simple good man in table fellowship with sinners (Mk 2:15–17). We see him helping people out even on Sunday (Lk 13:10–17). We find him attacking the religious leadership of his day for straining out gnats and swallowing camels, adhering fanatically to the traditions of their ancestors while neglecting justice and mercy and faith (Mt 23:23). We find him, not leading public prayers or gathering people for sacrifices, but quietly spending himself to free people from their burdens—their inner demons, their diseases, their guilt—and urging others to help. Just as tirelessly he bears witness to the truth, though he knows what happens sooner or later to people who bear witness to the truth.

Just as the great commandment summarizes his life and teaching in a verbal formula, the last supper epitomizes it in a symbolic action. In giving the bread and the wine, Jesus tries to compress into a pregnant gesture everything his life has meant. Anticipating his death on the next day, and wishing to make it clear that this death is something not imposed on him but freely chosen as the way he wants to express his love for his Father and us, he gives his disciples the bread and the wine, after giving thanks, and says: "This is my body for you." "This is my blood poured out for you." It is his own living of the great commandment, and he proposes it as the model for ours: "Do this in memory of me." What he intends is made further intelligible by two surrounding statements, both about choice.

> The ruler of this world is coming. He has no power over me; but I do as the Father has commanded me, so that the world may know that I love the Father. Rise, let us go (Jn 14:30–31).

> Greater love has no one than this, that a may lay down his life for his friends (Jn 15:13).

Jesus is the perfect embodiment of what he teaches. And the Eucharist, because it contains the summary of his teaching and his life, remains the sustaining ritual action of the Christian community.

Christian Growth Today

We have looked at the Word made flesh. Now we look at ourselves. The purpose of our lives is to become like Jesus, and not just to resemble him externally but to be rooted and grounded in him (Eph 3:17), to be ever more closely identified with him so that we can say, "I live, now not I, but Christ lives in me" (Gal 2:20). Any growth in the living out of the great commandment is growth in Christ. The entire object of Christian spirituality is right here.

To apply these foundational truths to the situation of the church today, we must advert to historical developments which produced the religious milieu in which most of us were raised. Until very recently, Christian spirituality had come to be commonly understood as the special preserve of a select number in the church, and it was conceived along ascetical lines. Vowed religious men and women and ordained priests were those who studied and lived Christian spirituality, while the great mass of Christians understood themselves as followers at a distance, people taught, ruled, and sanctified by these others. They kept the commandments and contributed to the support of the church. But they did not think of themselves as called to a serious life of prayer, to what might be called holiness, or to any kind of ministry in the church. What had insinuated itself into the body of Christ was a two-class mentality, whose foundations in the New Testament it would be very difficult to find.

Into this situation Vatican II spoke a revolutionary new word, which was really a very old word. In a departure from recent tradition, the Council played down the distinction between clergy, religious, and laity. It discontinued the language of "wholeheartedness" to characterize those who follow Christ in clerical or religious life, a usage which suggested that those who follow him in other styles of life are less than wholehearted. It used instead the expressions "more readily" and "more easily" to describe how those who are priests or religious can devote themselves to prayer and the apostolate. But it said nothing to suggest that these people are automatically holy just by reason of their state of life, or that those who are called along other Christian paths are automatically deprived of the opportunity for holiness by their circumstances.

The most important Council document, the *Dogmatic Constitution on the Church,* cornerstone of the whole conciliar achievement, is most instructive in its very outline. Instead of beginning, as previous treatments of the church have, with hierarchical organization and lines of authority, this document begins with biblical metaphors which describe the mystery of the whole church. The church is the coming Kingdom of God, a sheepfold, a land to be cultivated, the building of God, God's family, God's temple, the Holy City, spouse of Christ, body of Christ. The constitution's second chapter is a lengthy development of the biblical metaphor of the church as the people of God. It speaks of the priesthood of all the members, states that all without exception are called by the Lord to perfect holiness, describes the sacramental life which undergirds their life together, then speaks of the church's mission as a concern and activity involving all the members. It is not until the third chapter of the constitution that there is discussion of what had usually been at the head of the book, namely, office and authority in the church, the Holy Father, the college of bishops, priests and deacons. In the treatment of the Council, office and authority are seen as derived from and functioning within the whole church body rather than somehow being anterior and originating. The next two chapters of the constitution return again to broader themes, the fourth chapter devoted entirely to the laity, and the fifth to "The Universal Call to Holiness." Just to round out this structural analysis, we might note that the sixth chapter discusses religious, the seventh the pilgrim church, and the eighth the Blessed Virgin Mary. The point of the whole discussion is that the church is conceived by the Second Vatican Council much more comprehensively than it had been for a long time, the conciliar position being that all who belong to the church are called both to the fullness of Christian sanctity and to the apostolate. Just in case this last item should be missed, the Council issues a whole separate document entitled, *On the Apostolate of the Laity.* In the contemporary vision of the church, therefore, it is hardly adequate to think of the laity as a vast silent majority whose calling is to follow, to be ministered to, and to obey.

The unfortunate effect of the two-class mentality in the church was that it short-circuited immense amounts of spiritual energy, leaving all kinds of potential for sanctity untapped and countless gifts for ministry unused. The achievement of the Council has been to call this entire dormant portion of the church back to life, causing a widespread resurgence of interest in spirituality and the emergence of many new forms of ministry.

In the Concrete

All Christians are called to holiness, and the features of Christian holiness are clearly seen in the life and teaching of Jesus. There is only one basic Christian spirituality, speaking as much to lay-persons as to priests and religious, demanding the same central things of any life-style, in any life-circumstances. To what sorts of things, then, will the Christian helper be attentive in listening to the person who seeks growth?

Well, that religious sister does not represent Christian holiness very well, who although she spends many hours a day in the service of people, does not pray. She has made public profession as a Christian and engages in the apostolate of the church, but it is questionable how good her roots are and therefore how fruitful her ministry is. "Apart from me you can do nothing" (Jn 15:5). And that pastor does not represent Christian holiness very well who, although he is a priest and says his breviary and celebrates the liturgy every day, is not very open to receiving his parishioners or listening to them, who typically squelches rather than encourages the initiatives his people take in trying to promote the life of the church. He has not taken adequate account of the importance of love of neighbor in Christian growth, love shown in open hospitality, friendliness and encouragement. Nor does he show adequate sensitivity to the truth wherever it might be spoken. And that layman does not exemplify Christian maturity very well who, although he is regular in his church attendance, contributes to the support of the church, and is a member of the Holy Name Society, spends all the rest of his time trying to acquire a fortune for himself, like the man in the gospel who builds bigger barns (Lk 12:15–21). It may not be dishonest but has he heard that saying of Jesus: "It is easier for a camel to go through the eye of a needle than for a rich man to enter the kingdom of God?" (Mk 10:25). Where love of neighbor is concerned, has he taken account of the effect of his actions on other people? For it is not only in one-to-one relationships, but in every social structure, that we love or fail to love our neighbor. So much of human misery in the world today is rooted in unjust economic and social structures. And that Christian laywoman needs to do some important self-reflection, who, although she is a daily communicant and is conscientious in her responsibilities toward her family, stoutly maintains, and even works for organizations which maintain that people on welfare are simply lazy, that homosexuals do not deserve even civil rights, and that social activists and protesters are Communists. She lets unexamined assumptions rule fairly large areas of her social conduct, and allows prejudice and bias to stand in for actual association with the people she condemns, association which almost always shatters stereotypes and lets in amazing illuminations.

These are scattered examples, but they demonstrate that Christian holiness is a many-sided and high ideal and a lifetime project. It is not achieved easily, is not ensured within any style of life, and is subject to loss as well as gain over the years. Growth on any side of it promotes growth on all others, but, similarly, regression on any side of it works as a drag on the other sides, and a blind spot in any area is a serious hindrance to growth in other areas.

Paradoxically, the foundation of any growth is self-acceptance at the point where one is. Here both the self and the helper have a role to play, both needing to make that crucial act of acceptance. Sometimes the person cannot make it for him- or herself. We usually find it hard to love ourselves, conscious as we are of all our shortcomings. Someone else has to love us first. This, of course, is exactly what God is always trying to get across to us—that he does love us first and without any questions.

> This is the love that I mean—not that we loved God but that he first loved us and sent his Son to be the expiation of our sins (1 Jn 4:10).

But we frequently need to see this love incarnated in some human being who knows our story, and that is where the helper comes in, the earthen vessel mediating the good news. Self-acceptance does not, of course, guarantee growth, but it is the first and indispensable step. It grounds the conviction that the project is worthwhile, nay, possible; it tells us that we have materials to work with which could be turned into something.

With this foundation in place, and it may need to be firmed in place conversation after conversation, the work that needs to be done will vary from person to person. One person will need to be helped most in strengthening a life of prayer. Another person will need trust in God in the uncertainties of experience. Some couples need to overcome acquisitiveness and consumerism, and simplify their lives. Some parents need help in expanding love from the immediate circle of family and close friends to the wider circle of the whole varied human community. Some people need consciousness-raising about and motivation to correct unjust and life-destroying social and economic structures in our nation and in the world. A young man or woman might need assistance in integrating sexuality into responsible loving. Others will need help identifying and developing their own peculiar ministerial charisms. Sometimes people need help with personal issues of particular urgency at a given time—troublesome relationships, work problems, a particular suffering, the vocation question, difficulties in prayer, sexual identity, important decisions, preparation for death. Any circumstance or situation can be made capital of, particularly those which challenge and stretch the individual the most. Any crisis is a fertile seedbed for Christian growth. God the life-giver is present and active in all events, waiting on our cooperation. The norm for growth is always Jesus, who so beautifully embodies the ideal, and whose gift to us is his own enabling Spirit.

One final note. The Christian helper needs to realize that he or she is not only watching and promoting spiritual growth in the other, but necessarily also earnestly pursuing it in his or her own life. This is not only because we do God's work effectively in the measure that we are united to him, but also because we can hardly ask others to do what we will not take the trouble to do ourselves. Jesus never did. And any kind of helping is so largely a matter of modeling. One thinks of the words of Emerson: "What you are thunders so loud I cannot hear what you are saying." Yet even where our words are concerned, we affect others more sometimes by offhand or incidental remarks than we do by our most careful and concerted discourses. The quality of our offhand remarks is largely determined by the quality of our lives.

QUESTIONS FOR REFLECTION AND DISCUSSION

1. What, as you see it, are the main values Jesus tried to live?

2. What are the main emphases in Jesus' teaching?

3. Does complete commitment to Christ demand the life of the vows?

4. What is the relationship between a particular spirituality—Franciscan, Benedictine, Jesuit, etc.—and what we find in Jesus' life and teaching?

5. What kind of growth in the Christian life do you desire for yourself right now?

SUGGESTIONS FOR FURTHER READING

Vatican II	*Dogmatic Constitution on the Church*
Vatican II	*Decree on the Apostolate of the Laity*
Quentin Quesnell	*This Good News*
Rudolph Bultmann	*Jesus and the Word*

5. Prayer:
An Orientation

There is no theological subject more written about today than prayer. A look through the advertising of religious publishers, or a casual stroll through a religious goods store, is an encounter with an overwhelming spate of literature and tapes on the subject. The sheer volume is an indication of the interest of the matter in the contemporary church. It might also be a warning to the judicious writer to say no more. But ours is a special interest in the subject, and this interest shapes our orientation. We are interested in the *helper's* relation to a person inquiring about how to begin or how to persevere or how to grow in prayer. The present chapter deals with the question of motivation, the next chapter with method. In the present chapter, let us examine prayer in the biblical tradition, then survey the contemporary resurgence of interest, then suggest a basic attitude to prayer that will remove some of the most common obstacles to its success.

The urgency of the matter of prayer for that ongoing helping relationship we call spiritual direction is that direction makes little sense in the life of someone who is not praying. One of the differences we have noted between counseling and spiritual direction is that in counseling one talks out one's concerns with the counselor, whereas in spiritual direction one talks with a spiritual director about one's relationship with God. The conversation with God, and the desire to deepen it, is the presupposition of the conversation with the director. Prayer is the heart of the conversation with God. Confronted with a person seeking spiritual direction, a relationship which has growth in the Christian life as its specific goal, one of the director's first concerns will be: Does this person pray?

Models of Prayer

Prayer is as old as the religious instinct itself, and the Judaeo-Christian Bible is filled with examples of it. Men and women in the Bible pray in very different contexts and show considerable variety in the ways they approach prayer, but they all take prayer seriously. Abraham, the father of faith, is a man familiar with God. He is a listener in prayer and hears God's command to leave his land and then later to sacrifice his son. He also hears God's promises, the promise of numerous progeny and the promise of the land. Worship is central in his prayer, and he offers sacrifices to God at all the key points of his journey. Moses, the great leader of people, shows a love of deep solitude in his prayer, again and again ascending the mountain to meet God alone. Much of his prayer revolves around his struggle with the demands of his difficult vocation. Jeremiah the prophet, another man on a demanding mission, is perfectly straight with God in prayer. He pours out his hurt, his frustrations, even his inner rebellion at the things God asks him to do. Esther's prayer is supplicatory. She prays on behalf of the Hebrew people before she takes her petition to the king of Persia. Trust is important in the prayer of Judith, who exhorts her beleaguered people to trust in God, and then utters a lengthy prayer before undertaking her dangerous mission to the enemy general. Each of these individuals is conscious of a mission from God and of the necessity of God's help in carrying it out, and this drives each to prayer. Each prays in his or her own way.

The Psalms are the prayer book of the Old Testament. Written by various persons over a long period of time, they exhibit the perennial prayer themes of the human heart. "God, I am utterly amazed at the splendor of your creation." "Lord, where are you now

that I need you?" "O God, I am sorry for what I have done."
"Lord, thank you for the gift of life." "Great God, I worship you."
"Lord, I trust you and wait for your deliverance, remembering all
you have done for me." "I thirst for you, O God."

This is the tradition in which Jesus is raised, and it is Luke who
is especially sensitive to Jesus' prayer-life. He shows us Jesus at
prayer at his baptism, during the night before the choice of the
Twelve, on the mountain when he is transfigured, in the garden before his passion, and at various times either early in the morning or
late at night. Jesus seems to be driven partly by a sense of need, partly by a great love for his Father, to deepen in prayer the union which
is the wellspring of his whole existence. It is this union which makes
his words the Father's words and his deeds the Father's deeds. Of
the content of his prayer we know very little. In his teaching on the
subject, he talks much more about the prayer of petition than about
the prayer of union, and urges the importance of prayer much more
than he deals with method. Perhaps he assumes we all know how to
pray, if we can just be persuaded to do it. He seems to view prayer
in a functional perspective, as an ingredient in a whole way of life
rather than as an end in itself. It is with the way of life that he is
concerned, as we saw in the last chapter.

What the Old Testament and New Testament inculcate and exemplify is carried on conspicuously by the great men and women of
Christian history. You could pick any of them at random—Bernard,
Benedict, Francis of Assisi, Clare, Teresa of Avila, John of the Cross,
Theresa of Lisieux, Ignatius Loyola, Catherine of Siena, Francis Xa-
vier—and find prayer an important part both of their lives and of
their writings. Methods differ, and the lives issuing from prayer vary
even more, but the taproot is the same. Closer to our own time we
could cite Simone Weil, Pierre Teilhard, Bonhoeffer, Mother Teresa.
Among our contemporaries, if we ask those whose lives impress us
with their spiritual vitality and gentle power, we usually find that
they take time for prayer.

What is true of the Judaeo-Christian tradition is true as well of
the great religions of the East. In fact, much of the present interest
in prayer and meditation has been inspired, or at least enriched, by
the Hindu, Buddhist, and Sufi traditions.

It is fascinating to see this contemporary resurgence of personal prayer in the West, particularly when one considers how common-place are descriptions of Western culture in terms of growing secu-larization. It seems to be a kind of spontaneous movement, flourishing to a great extent outside the ambience of organized re-ligion, arising evidently from felt need. Many of our young people are teaching us how vital quiet time is to any kind of personal in-teriority in a culture characterized by so much frenetic activity. We need to take time out, they say. We need to get centered, to be at home with ourselves, to open up and live within our own sacred tem-ple, to be attuned to the deeper voice and the more profound direc-tion, to find a source of peace inside ourselves. Otherwise, we are simply swept from one thing to another, without knowing who we are or what we want or what lies below the surfaces of life in this world. This is a message our age needs to hear, even those of us who may be habitual churchgoers. It seems a shame that until recently, we Christians have shared so little of our rich contemplative heritage with most believers, with the result that many of our people know only how to recite formulary prayers, make spontaneous prayers of petition, and frequent the sacraments. People today are clearly de-sirous of more. This is a golden opportunity for the Christian helper, whether youth minister, visitor to the sick and dying, or spiritual di-rector.

Motives for Prayer

We are surrounded by living examples, and they extend back through a long tradition. But you might still ask: Why should I pray? Let us look at two simple reasons why you might want to. One is need. The other is love.

We saw need at work in the Old Testament models we consid-ered, and in the life of Jesus. It shaped the prayer of each. Maybe you feel weak in the face of your life's responsibilities. You feel the stresses of growing up, the loneliness of being single, the challenge of being celibate, the difficulty of loving your husband or wife, the problems of raising your children, the strain involved in your job. You are not sure how to meet the many people that you meet, how to answer their questions, bear their burdens, love them as they are, minister to their griefs, open their eyes to aspects of life they are not seeing. Perhaps you might be concerned about a particular person at a particular time, and want to hold him or her up to the Lord. Or it might be a particular crisis in your own development that becomes thematic in prayer for a while. You are doing good, but are not sure how much longer you can keep doing good, and you need prayer to sustain your effort. You do daily battle with weaknesses and temptations, and sorely feel the need for some assistance from somewhere. It may be drink or drugs. It may be fear, or sex, or anger, or self-pity. Maybe you are confused about the direction your life should be taking. You are going through a "passage" and need help to find your way. You are feeling dissatisfaction with your present pattern and sense a call within to something more, and you need to bring that to clarity before God. Perhaps you have to make a major decision. It may be about a job, a relationship, your vocation, your priorities. These are some of the needs from which prayer takes its rise, and to which it owes its peculiar character.

There are other needs too, of a different sort. Maybe you feel the need for someone to thank for the gift of your life. Maybe you feel deeply that someone should be praised for the ocean and the mountains, the rose and the snow, the leopard and the hummingbird, the baby at the breast, the romping little girl, the gracious host, the kindly old man. Maybe you feel you would like to thank someone for your health, your talents, your virtues, the things you have accomplished, the help you can give to others, the friends who have been given to you, the way perfectly dreadful experiences have brought greater depth and new life to you. These too are needs of the heart from which prayer arises. We saw some of them expressed in the psalms. G. K. Chesterton came to his conversion out of a felt necessity to be able to give someone thanks.

If the first reason to pray is need, the second is love. Perhaps you want to pray just because you like to pray, because there is no better company on the face of the earth than the profoundly quiet company of God. Maybe prayer is a passion with you, as it was with the saints, and you are bitten by it and cannot get over it. You go to prayer daily, seeking God as the great mystery to which you are so deeply drawn, and you do it even though the effort seems often so fruitless and dreadfully dry. Sometimes you have to live on memories, memories of past visitations, moments when God seemed very close, everything was good, and life was profoundly meaningful. Then your prayer is waiting and hoping, on the strength of these experiences. Other times your whole day, or a series of days, will be palpably filled with the presence, and punctuated by clear signs of a particular providence. Love for this mysterious benefactor moves you to seek quiet time to be alone with him. This is the other great motive out of which prayer springs. You simply love the God you know, and want to be with him.

> Ho, everyone who thirsts, come to the waters, and you who have no money, come, buy and eat! Come, buy wine and milk without money and without price. Why do you spend your money for that which is not bread, and your labor for that which does not satisfy? Hearken diligently to me, and eat what is good, and delight yourself in fatness. Incline your ear and come to me; hear that your soul may live; and I will make with you an everlasting covenant (Is 55:1–3).

If a person feels either of these, a need for God or a love for him, there is no need to persuade that person to pray. But if these things, singly or together, are not part of a person's experience, talk about or exhortation to prayer, or even making prayer part of a daily rule, are not going to make much difference. The effort will not be long sustained, because the desire does not come from within. Helping people to pray is a matter of helping them find the starting points in their lives, the needs and the enthusiasms already there to be tapped, and then helping them shape their prayer accordingly, so that it is really their own.

The Basic Stance

The first principle of prayer is to be yourself. Prayer is being yourself before God. This may sound obvious, but it bears a little developing.

Many people would like to pray, but feel they do not know how. Prayers of petition they can handle, and brief ejaculations or slightly longer formulary prayers they can learn and recite, but in the deeper waters of meditation or contemplation they feel very insecure. How should they begin?

By analogy, how do you learn to talk with or be with another human being? Do you begin completely ignorant and have to learn every step of a proper procedure? Or are the instincts and inclinations already in place, so that you can begin easily enough and grow in facility through experience? The latter description better captures the reality, and what holds true of human interpersonal relationships applies also to the relationship with God. The first principle is simply to be yourself, and let it happen. But people wonder if this is good enough, and that is where the trouble begins.

A lot of prayer is defeated by pseudo ideals. One ready way to misconceive it is to think of it as making something beautiful for God. You will think good and holy thoughts. You will have warm and loving feelings. You will say things which please God, and this will be your prayer. It will be a gift. That does not seem like a bad idea, but it often proves to be quite taxing in practice. The good thoughts do not come, and the good feelings are nowhere to be found. You can think of nothing to say. And so, after a few days of this, you give up, concluding that you must not have the gift of prayer.

Or a slight variant. You do not have quite such grandiose expectations about what you could make for God. You may conceive of prayer more as something you need, and without looking for particularly inspired thoughts or intense feelings, would just like to be able to remain attentive so as to get the most out of it. So you close your eyes and try to lay aside all that pertains to your ordinary life, to be in stillness with God. But distractions pour in on you relentlessly. One thought after another pulls you away from the business at hand. And so again, after a few attempts, you decide that nothing is coming of this and give it up.

You might go in with a different expectation and hope. This one is common in retreats. You seek a religious experience—maybe not a vision or revelation, but at least a strong experience of God's presence and love. And you figure this will grow stronger gradually as time goes on. So you embark on your course. You have no religious experience. Instead God seems distant and disinterested, and you struggle to make contact, feeling alone and rejected.

These are deeply disappointing experiences, and they have done in many a fledgling. Others do not give up so easily. The hardy will persevere at it for a year, sometimes more than that, and their cessation may be gradual rather than sudden and complete, taking the form of postponing rather than simply stopping prayer. But the postponements lead again and again to prayer being pushed out of the day, as the convenient time never seems to come. The reason, of course, is that one does not really want to pray. It is just too hard and too apparently unproductive. The experience of disillusionment has eaten away at the heart, and one has laid the project aside.

The problem, the helper must bear in mind, is not really personal failure but pseudo ideals. Prayer is not making something beautiful for God, or having God make something beautiful for you, or getting into a separate space where your life cannot touch you. All the living models of prayer we have considered show us that prayer is rather being yourself before God, coming as you are, dialoging with him from your present situation, not putting on a face and manufacturing appropriate thoughts and feelings, but being yourself and working with the thoughts and feelings that are there.

> What shall I do with this people? They are almost ready to stone me! (Moses—Ex 17:4).

> You have duped me, O Lord, and I let myself be duped. You are stronger than I, and you have prevailed, and I have become a laughing stock all the day (Jer 20:7).

> I loathe my life: I would not live forever. Let me alone, for my days are a breath . . . How long will you not look away from me, nor let me alone till I swallow my spittle? If I sin, what do I do to you, you watcher of persons? Why have you made me your mark? (Job 7:16–20).

> How long, O Lord, will you utterly forget me? How long will you hide your face from me? How long must I bear pain in my soul, and have sorrow in my heart all the day? (Ps 13).

Not all one's thoughts and feelings are negative, of course. But the point needs emphasizing that the negative ones are as acceptable as the positive. Prayer is being oneself before God. The most illuminating analogy for understanding it is the classical analogy of friendship. This analogy and its ramifications are the subject of the next chapter.

QUESTIONS FOR REFLECTION AND DISCUSSION

1. Why do you suppose prayer is so important in the bibilical tradition, in both Old and New Testaments?

2. What is your own thumbnail description of prayer?

3. Why do you pray? (Or why don't you?)

4. How do you pray?

5. How do the two motives for prayer named in this chapter relate to your own motives?

6. How would you deal with a person who came to you and said: "I know I should pray, but somehow I never get around to it"?

SUGGESTIONS FOR FURTHER READING.

Karl Rahner   *Encounters with Silence*

Edward Farrell   *Prayer is a Hunger*

Louis Evely   *Our Prayer*

Louis Evely   *We Dare To Say Our Father*

6. Prayer: Helping Someone Grow in It

A friend is a person with whom you can afford to be yourself. Just yourself, nothing more or less. That is enough. There are plenty of people in the world with whom you cannot afford to be quite yourself. You have to present the proper face, make the right impression. For them you may have to make something beautiful, or attempt to. With them, you need to be strong and have yourself together; at least you would like to appear that way. With a friend, none of this is necessary. When you meet others, you need to have some energy, to be "up for it." With a friend, you do not really need that. You can open the door to a friend even when you are a wreck and could not turn on the charm if you wanted to.

Is not God such a friend as this? Does he not love you as much as these others do for the person you simply are? Is there any point in trying to put on a proper face for someone who knows you as well as God? To be with a friend is simply to be oneself. If the analogy holds, and it has long been in use in the Christian prayer tradition, then we can go to prayer as we are, and the matter of our communication with God might turn out to be anything at all—and some days not much of anything. Probably some days we will do more of the talking, and other days God probably will. Such is the nature of communication between two persons who are on familiar terms.

Starting with the Word

This last is a strange statement. Does God speak, and if he does, what does it sound or feel like? How do I know when he wants to speak, so that I can listen? And if he might really speak to me, how would I know it was he and not just my imagination? This question of who speaks and when is an important one in prayer. If prayer is interpersonal communication, presumably there will be something said by both parties. When and how does God speak? Or is prayer, after all, just my pouring countless things day after day into the ear of God?

One of the cardinal principles of prayer is that God does speak and always speaks first. Prayer then is what I say, and it is always a response to him. Now that is already quite a reversal of the common presumption, that the initiative in prayer is mine, that I seek out God and talk to him after I have learned a method for doing so, and he just silently takes it all in. It is truer to say that the reason I want to pray at all is that God has spoken to me and I want to speak to him in response. But where does this speaking of his take place?

One answer would seem to be scripture, and some people suggest that prayer should always begin with a passage of scripture, and proceed as a reflection on and response to it. This is good. Scripture is indeed the word of God, and it is not a dead word either. Though it was written in the past and is to a great extent a record of things past, it is a word which comes to life when it is read today or any time, since our God is a living God and the revelation he has made of himself in scripture is a revelation of who he is always and what his attitude toward us is yesterday, today, and forever (Heb 13:8). So scripture is a very appropriate starting point for prayer, and furnishes superb material for reflection and affective response. We sometimes experience it as quite clearly a living word of God spoken to us this day; it really does mediate his presence and action to us, and makes our prayer quite easy. So scripture is surely part of the answer to our question about the respective roles of God and ourselves in prayer.

But is it the entire answer? Does a person who does not read the Bible hear no word of God at all? Then the majority of the earth's people hear no word. And what shall I do when scripture does not speak to me though I read it with the greatest attention? What shall I do when I start with a passage and have no sooner finished reading it than my mind is on something else, and even repeated returns to the text will not make my mind stick there? Is that the end of my prayer? Is there no place else where God speaks?

The Word of God in Nature and History

The Hebrews, as we saw, knew God before they had the Bible. They wrote the Bible as the record of their experience of him. They record two primary types of experience. They encounter God in history, or in the events of their lives; and they encounter him in nature, or creation, terms which designate all that is. They come to recognize the reality of God and the quality of his relationship to them as they go through various experiences and find him always a savior. This discovery of his lordship of history leads gradually to the realization that he must be the creator and sustainer of all things as well.

Out of these experiences of him, they wrote their scriptures or holy books. But this means that the experience of God is larger than the Bible and certainly prior to it. This may recall some of the ideas we saw earlier, about God as the depth in things or as the horizon of all experience—God present and active everywhere. The Bible is one people's diary of this. It has special value for all those people whose faith is shaped by the Judaeo-Christian tradition. But it is surely not the first or only word God has ever spoken, nor did he fall silent when its last book was completed. This has crucial implications for prayer.

The God who spoke in the lives of those people long ago speaks also in mine, and is just as present and active for me as he was for them, quite apart from written words. If the word of God in nature and history is an appropriate starting point for prayer, I might legitimately start my prayer from significant points in my own nature and history. I can begin from my own nature and history. I can begin from my own deep longing for life, my experience of my work, the important relationships in my world, the things I most wonder at, the restlessness and loneliness of my heart, my experiences of power and achievement, a painful conversation still fresh and smarting, a recent gift of love. These things, which from a less adequate perspective are looked upon as "distractions" from prayer, turn out to be the very stuff of prayer. For all the events of my life somehow bear God's word to me, and to mull them in search of their significance in him is to listen and respond to his word in as true a sense as to reflect on a passage of scripture. Scripture records salvation history. My own salvation history is now being written. What Luke says in a summary statement concerning Mary serves as an excellent paradigm for prayer: "Mary kept all these things, pondering them in her heart" (Lk 2:19). What things? The things that were happening to her. Luke makes the remark twice, the first time of the experience of the coming of the shepherds at Jesus' birth, the second of the experience of losing Jesus in Jerusalem. Both of them happened too fast and were too startling to be plumbed in all their significance on the spot. So Mary kept them in her heart and pondered them. This is prayer as response not to scripture but to a word of God spoken in the events of one's life.

It was, we recall, not only in history but in nature as well that the Hebrews encountered God. This is the theological underpinning of the kind of prayer that arises spontaneously in the presence of mountains or the sea, in park or woods, at sunrise or sunset, on fishing and camping trips, at the sight of beautiful flowers, animals, persons. "In him we live and move and have our being" (Acts 17:28). Persons with this sort of contemplative bent should be encouraged to make the most of it as their point of departure for prayer.

When people speak of trouble in prayer, they should be asked what they enjoy, what they marvel at, what they suffer from, where they experience depth. That is the point where God speaks to them, and from which their prayer can take its rise. Calling such things distractions is the worst possible interpretation of them.

Prayer is simply being with these things, whether from nature or history, open to the mystery of God in them. Prayer is being ourselves with God, with our lives and experiences, attentive to the words of God's self-manifestation in them, his care, his beauty, his call, his peace, his challenge. The experience will at times be one of deep feeling. More commonly it will be quite low-keyed, like the day-to-day sharings of a long-standing friendship. It works best when one is quite alert. But it is not impossible when one is tired, since it is simply a matter of being oneself, not of making something beautiful, and something is better than nothing. Sometimes it will focus on a present object, sometimes on a recent event. Sometimes it will entertain the whole panorama of one's life. Sometimes it will be a very simple being together without much talking. The analogy of friendship helps us to recognize and be at peace with each of these modalities.

Finding One's Style

The analogy of friendship helps us understand another aspect of prayer. If prayer is being oneself with God, then each of us will pray a little differently. The glory that the rose reflects back to God is not the same as the glory of the daffodil. What we love in a friend is that friend's uniqueness—the peculiar tilt of the head, the movement of the hands, the smile, the tone of the voice, the expressions of the face. God rejoices in these same particularities when each of us prays. We can learn much from John of the Cross, Teresa of Avila, Ignatius Loyola where prayer is concerned. But when the broad hints have been taken, their prayer is theirs and ours is ours. The trick where method is concerned is to find the method that suits us. The task of a spiritual director is not to teach a particular method, but to help persons find the approach which best suits them. If they ask how they are supposed to pray, the best answer is: "How would you like to pray?" If they are having trouble, the first thing to look for is ways in which they have straight-jacketed themselves in someone else's method. Individual style is the key, with freedom and spontaneity. Thus, some people do yoga first and then sit composed on the floor. Some like nothing better than to walk. Some are drawn to the Blessed Sacrament. Some like to focus on a cross, statue, or candle when they pray. Others like to play the guitar and sing their prayer; still others pray in tongues. Some like to lie prostrate; some just sit in their chairs; others prefer to kneel. Some start with scripture; some begin with the rosary in their hands; some begin nowhere in particular. Some will use psalms; some open meditation books; some let the Jesus Prayer or other ejaculation or mantra serve as a rhythm to keep them centered. Some will let persons about whom they are concerned pass through their minds; others will leave everything to God and just try to be with him; still others will do now the one, now the other. There is no one way. There are countless ways. One's individuality is the signature on one's worship of God.

A Critical Juncture

There is one transition or passage in prayer for which the helper should be especially watchful. That is the passage from activity to receptivity. John of the Cross makes much of it, because he is convinced that going with this evolution rather than resisting it is essential to one's development in prayer. To understand the transition, the analogy of friendship is again helpful. In a friendship, there is a natural movement from more activity to more passivity or receptivity. At the beginning of a relationship there is more need to talk, to explain oneself, to stir the coals. As time goes on, this sort of thing becomes less necessary. The relationship is established, the persons understand one another without need of too many cues, and time can be spent together quite easily and richly in relatively wordless communion. So it is in the relationship with God. As familiarity grows, it is attended by a movement toward simplification.

Something in us resists this. Perhaps we do not expect any development in our relationship with God, which, after all, is not exactly the same as other relationships. Perhaps our feeling about our prayer is that the tie with God in it is already tenuous enough, the experience of contact too faint as it is, without decreasing our activity. If we stopped speaking, would anyone speak? If we stopped turning over reflections, would anything happen at all? How much silence can a person take? These are reasonable grounds for hesitation, and it is true that one can too quickly abandon one's activity and move toward a quietism which is not fruitful. But one can err on the side of safety also, maintaining a bustle that blocks development. For most people of prayer, this latter is the greater danger.

The sign a spiritual director should be alert to in the prayer of one who is going through this transition under the action of the Spirit is that the old tried and true methods simply will not work any-more. The mind cannot concentrate; the familiar feelings no longer arise; the text goes dead. The person is surprised and usually be-comes discouraged, because what had always worked so well works no longer. These are the signs which point to the need to take a less active, more receptive, approach to prayer, to put matter and con-sideration aside and move in the direction of a prayer of quiet, simple regard, loving attention.

This is not always so easy to do. One feels very insecure, like a person adrift, and wonders if anything is going on at all. One is strongly tempted to turn back, to seize the initiative again and try to get something going by diligent effort. People in this stage of de-velopment often feel very anxious and fearful that they are displeas-ing God. This in itself is a sign that the movement is from God, not a personal choice of the free and easy path. It is in this distressing time that a director can be of great help, just by acquainting the per-son with this common and necessary transitional experience and by giving him or her permission to stop flailing the arms and relax. The director can gently support and encourage as the person learns to be comfortable with God's ways of quiet copresence and understated leadings. It is a vital service, opening a new vista.

Carl Jung speaks in psychological terms of the task of the first half of life and the task of the second. His analysis corresponds per-fectly to this division of the spiritual life into active and receptive phases. In the first half of life, we are more inclined to see the world as a thing to be mastered, our lives as something to be taken hold of and steered in definite directions. We must make our way in the world, discover and exploit our talents, find our place and make our mark. We are ambitious, active, eager to control, make, and accom-plish. Our gaze is directed outward. Then we come to the second half of life. Those tasks are now accomplished, and our powers are be-ginning to wane. We have learned that life is a mysterious process which happens to us while we are making other plans, and that it shapes us more than we shape it. If our development is normal and healthy, our concern focuses more on our inner selves now, and we want to foster an inner life that our earlier outward activity had held in check. It is the same in the spiritual life. At first we seem to be in control. Then God takes the control from us, increasingly hollow-

7. Christian Choices: An Orientation

One of the areas in which those who seek God in their lives need help is the making of important choices. To live is to choose; to live a Christian life is to choose in the Lord. Jesus was always concerned with choices. "The things that are pleasing to him, I do always" (Jn 8:29). "My meat is to do the will of the one who sent me, to accomplish his work" (Jn 4:34). He was concerned about it for us too.

> Not everyone who says to me "Lord, Lord" shall enter the kingdom of heaven, but the person who does the will of my Father who is in heaven (Mt 7:21).

In the life of Jesus, there seems to be something more involved than just keeping the commandments. We see him struggling in the desert with subtle temptations where his work as messiah is concerned, sifting out the way his Father wanted him to accomplish the task from the more immediately plausible methods of using dramatic gestures or employing political power (Mt 4:1–11). We see him turning down the suggestion of his brothers that he go up to the feast in Jerusalem to manifest himself to the people, electing instead to go up later in secret (Jn 7:1–10). We observe him escaping the violence of the people (Lk 4:28–30), and eluding arrest on occasion (Jn 7:30), but then freely yielding himself to his captors when his hour has come (Jn 14:30–31). We find him at prayer in the garden, struggling with the difficulty of that momentous decision (Lk 22:39–46), as we found him at prayer the night before he made his choice of the Twelve (Lk 6:12–16). His actions suggest that there is a particular divine leading within the broader context of generally recognized good and evil, for which the religious individual listens closely. Thus Abraham hears the call to leave his land, Moses to lead his people out of bondage, Jeremiah to be a prophet, Jesus to suffer and die for us all. It is the individual destiny which must be discerned within a broad religious framework of life, that the formative choices of one's existence may be in the Lord.

Sometimes it is a question of a vocation in the classical sense—to marriage, religious life, priesthood. But there are other important choices too. Shall we put mother in a nursing home, or take care of her here? Shall I accept the promotion that would mean our leaving this place and moving to another city? Shall we have another child? Shall I accede to my community's request that I be superior? What should my field of specialization be? What are the service works that have the best claim on my or our time and energy? Shall I involve myself in demonstrations and protests which are in violation of civil law? What is appropriate sexual expression in a particular relationship? How much time shall I give to prayer? Shall I stay with this marriage? Shall I remain in religious life? Shall I have the special life-support systems removed, and die? In these and other important matters, one wants to know God's will, to lift choice above personal whimsy and make it in the Lord. But how does one find God's will? What the Christian helper needs when he or she is asked to assist in such situations is a basic orientation and some methodological guidelines. Let us first establish the orientation.

The Freedom of the Children of God

The Christian economy is an economy of freedom. The point has sometimes been lost. If we go back to the prescriptions of Jesus for the life God wants us to live, what we find is simple and basic, with the particulars left up to ourselves. The Father of Jesus Christ is not a God of constraints but a God of freedom. He takes our maturity seriously, and, after a few simple directives, leaves our lives in our own hands.

Jesus enjoined but one commandment: Love God with your whole heart, and love your neighbor as yourself. This, he said, summarizes all that is said in the law and the prophets (Mt 22:37–40). In another formulation, he says: "A new commandment I give to you, that you love one another even as I have loved you" (Jn 13:34). This sets the tone of a whole life. For more particular guidance, one is instructed to look within to the abiding presence of the Holy Spirit. The Spirit helps us know the demands of love in particular situations.

> These things I have spoken to you while I am still with you. But the Counselor, the Holy Spirit, whom the Father will send in my name, he will teach you all things, and bring to your remembrance all that I have said to you (Jn 14:25–26).

> I have yet many things to say to you, but you cannot bear them now. When the Spirit of truth comes, he will guide you into all the truth; for he will not speak on his own authority, but whatever he hears he will speak, and he will declare to you the things that are to come (Jn 16:12–13).

So the Spirit will be active in our lives, extending Jesus' own teaching and guidance in a living and concrete way. This, then, is the basic equipment for the moral and spiritual life of the Christian: Jesus' great commandment, and the living guidance of the Holy Spirit.

Paul echoes this orientation of Jesus, and calls even more attention to being led by the Spirit. He too states that there is only one commandment in the new dispensation, a single law summing up and dispensing with all the rest (Rm 13:8–10; Gal 5:14; Col 3:14). Like Jesus, he looks to the Spirit to help us make that commandment concrete in the circumstances of our lives.

> But now we are discharged from the law, dead to that which held us captive, so that we serve not under the old written code but in the new life of the Spirit (Rm 7:6).

> If we live by the Spirit, let us also walk by the Spirit (Gal 5:25).

> For those who live according to the flesh set their minds on the things of the flesh, but those who live according to the Spirit set their minds on the things of the Spirit (Rm 8:5).

The only trouble with this way of living the religious life is that it is rather insecure. It becomes very difficult to enjoy certitude that one is really doing the right thing and pleasing God. So the human drive for security and self-justification takes over and buries the original teaching under multiple new additions. It seeks refuge in more laws, in living authorities, or in methods of divination. Let us take a brief look at each.

False Securities

The Old Testament is well known for the legalistic approach to being right and pleasing God. More and more laws were written, until the finest details of life were provided for—what to eat and what not to eat, when and how to wash one's hands, what to wear, precisely what penalty to exact for any breach of law, how the temple should be furnished and how the ritual should be performed in every particular. This was the scene onto which Jesus walked, and he showed himself a somewhat freer spirit where purification, Sabbath observance, capital punishment, and other issues were concerned. In one especially vigorous denunciation of the scribes and pharisees, he points to the problem the legalistic approach fosters.

> Woe to you, scribes and pharisees, hypocrites! For you tithe mint and dill and cummin, and have neglected the weightier matters of the law, justice and mercy and faith; these you ought to have done without neglecting the others.

> You blind guides, straining out a gnat and swallowing a
> camel! (Mt 23:23–24).

And again:

> This people honors me with their lips, but their hearts are
> far from me. In vain do they worship me, teaching as doc-
> trines the precepts of human beings (Mk 7:6–7).

When Paul reflects on the work of Jesus, he summarizes it more
than once by saying that Jesus has freed us from the law (Gal 3:10–
14, 23–26; 4:4–7; 5:1, 13–14). Yet, before we have gone very far at
all down the road of Christian history, the law is back again. Now
it is not Old Testament law but the precepts of moral theology and
the prescriptions of canon law, which again attempt to legislate the
particulars of God's demand, providing for all possible contingen-
cies. It is only recently that a protest against this imposing and still
growing body of law has been raised, and the church reflects again
on the purpose and limits of law.

Law is not the only defense against insecurities and the burden
of freedom. There are also living authorities. You can get yourself
a guru, a confessor, a spiritual director who will tell you what to do.
In the Old Testament, people went to the scribes for the correct interpretation of the law. In the church, we have had a good deal of
paternalism with child-like dependence in all matters of moral decision. Particularly in Roman Catholicism, it was believed in a very
unnuanced kind of way that when the hierarchy spoke, God spoke.
This can be a tyrannous regime, but it is another refuge from the
burden of freedom and responsibility.

Now that the church is moving back to freedom, and culture is
less sure of itself than it was, we see growing numbers of people taking refuge in various fundamentalist and authoritarian religions and
quasi-religions, led by strong individuals who are happy to take over
people's responsibilities for them and tell them exactly what to believe and do. A community of the like-minded adds a strong sense
of belonging, answering another profound human need. The community reinforces the prevailing ideology, giving a deep sense that: "We
are right. We have the light. Those who disagree with us are under

the power of the devil." It amounts to a kind of brainwashing, and is protected by strict censorship. Jonestown in Guyana is the most dramatic, but by no means the only, contemporary instance of this sort of group. Certitude and community constitute their lure. Authority is the key to both.

Vatican II seems to be acknowledging the church's excessive reliance on authority and to be setting a new orientation, really the original orientation, when, in its *Declaration on Religious Freedom,* it states:

> This freedom means that all persons are to be immune from coercion on the part of individuals or of social groups and of any human power, in such wise that in matters religious no one is to be forced to act in a manner contrary to his or her own beliefs (#2). Hence every person has the duty, and therefore the right, to seek the truth in matters religious, in order that he or she may with prudence form for himself right and true judgments of conscience with the use of all suitable means (#3).

> Revelation discloses the dignity of the human person in its full dimensions. It gives evidence of the respect which Christ showed toward the freedom with which each person is to fulfill his or her duty of belief in the Word of God (#9).

The third false solution to the problem of freedom is somewhat less appealed to. Its broad name is divination. It looks for signs, for portents in the skies, for clues in tea leaves or the entrails of birds. It employs augurs, fortune tellers, and astrologers. We may think of these methods as primitive. But the expectation returns in a subtler form in some approaches to spiritual discernment. The hope is magical: If I can just get the formula down, and use it without a flaw, I will get an infallible hold on God's will for me. Now discernment is a good thing, and it is discernment we are considering in the present chapter. But when discernment is understood as divination, it is misconceived, and is freighted with expectations it cannot meet.

The point of this lengthy discussion on freedom in the context of discernment is to serve as a guide to the spiritual director. When someone asks for assistance in making important choices, the director should realize that the appeal to law, the assumption of personal authority over the other's life, and the use of discernment as a kind of magical method with infallible results are all based on poor theology. If God has given us a genuine gift of freedom in the lives we live before him, given direction only by the great commandment and the living presence of the Spirit within us, there must be some other approach to the making of good choices.

God's Will

What has been said about God's program of life for us as it is lived out and taught by Jesus gives us the key to understanding the question of God's will.

The will of God has sometimes been presented as fixed from all eternity. God has conceived the shape of each person's life, and has a will for the details of each person's path. He also foreknows what each person is going to do in every particular. Yet it has been maintained that we are free. The combination has always been a conundrum to the reflective.

Process theology, stemming chiefly from Alfred North Whitehead, but further developed by several others, makes a significantly different presentation of the matter in the present century, and has won much theological support because it seems to make better sense of this and other difficult problems in a perspective more congenial to contemporary modes of thought. To present the matter very simply, process theology speaks rather of God's purpose than of God's will. God's purpose for each of us is that we reach the fullness of our personal potential. God's purpose for the world is very similar. It is evolution toward the fullness of human community. Put more in the language of the gospel, God's purpose for each of us is that we become mature, balanced, free, and loving; that our lives be rooted in faith, hope, and charity; that we live as Jesus lived. That is the fullness of personal potential. His purpose for the world is that it become his kingdom—a kingdom of justice and peace, of truth and holiness. The specifics involved in these projects are left to human choice, operating within the context of the lure of God's purpose.

The goal of the Christian life is to imitate and follow Jesus, who is the way and the truth and the life. But what does it mean to imitate Jesus? Does it mean I should be a carpenter? An itinerant preacher? A celibate? A man? Does it mean I should be a healer, or give bread to the multitudes? Does it mean I should die on the cross? It might mean one or other of these, but it does not necessarily mean any of them. It rather means that I should live the values of Jesus, base my life on his great commandment, be led by the same Spirit. I could do it in Chicago or Tampa, in Dublin, Tel Aviv, or Moscow. I could do it as man or woman, as single or married, as nurse, social worker, homemaker, artist, monk, mechanic, or scholar. Those judgments God leaves to me. He does not know what I will choose until I choose it, because I am genuinely free and therefore also unpredictable. Jung says that to imitate Christ does not mean to do everything he did, but to live out our own individual destiny as authentically and wholeheartedly as he lived out his. The specifics of my following of Jesus, therefore, will flow from my own personality, my talents, attractions, and opportunities, and from the signs of the times.

If this is a fair presentation of the matter, we would go about the process of discernment differently than we would on some other theological readings of God's will. We would be trying not to sniff out the hidden preplan by a method of discovery, but to make the best creative choice we can make in any given set of circumstances. God presents us with a blank check rather than with a check awaiting only our signature. When we say, "God, what do you want me to do?" he says, "Freedom is my gift to you, and judgment. You know that I want life for you. Be all you can be. Do all you can do. I have given you my Son as a model, and I have given you our Spirit. Make whatever choices and decisions seem good to you."

On this interpretation, Abraham shaped his own life within the broad framework of God's purpose, and Moses shaped his journey through the wilderness. Paul mapped out his own itinerary, choosing these cities rather than those, and adopted the style of life he judged appropriate for the achievement of his goals. Ignatius reshaped religious life because the existing forms did not quite suit his vision and objectives, again making decisions and choices within the broad framework of God's purpose. Martin Luther King made other judgments and choices, and Dorothy Day still others. Mother Teresa of Calcutta, hearing the same basic call, has made yet other determinations, again involving innovation and doubtless based on her personality, talents, attractions, opportunities, and the signs of the times as she reads them. Each is a cocreator with God, endowed with much autonomy.

There must be a way of living in the plains of liberty with a reasonable degree of assurance that we are what God would have us be, without dependence on laws, authorities, or divination. Is there any way of refining the process by which one makes important judgments and elections so that they are more surely guided by God's purpose? How can we more readily find the movement of the Spirit in our own lives? It is to this that we now turn our attention.

QUESTIONS FOR REFLECTION AND DISCUSSION

1. What is meant by the term "discernment"?

2. How do you know that you yourself are following God's will for your life?

3. Could a person who left a Christian marriage, or who married after taking religious vows or accepting ordination, possibly be doing God's will?

4. Does God have a will for me that I marry this person rather than another?

5. If Jesus has freed us from the law, how do you account for the development of so much legislation in the church?

6. Someone comes to you and says: "My husband and I are wondering if we should have another child. We want to do God's will in the matter. How can we find God's will?" How would you help this person?

7. A young man in his twenties comes to you and says: "From time to time I wonder if I should enter religious life. How does a per-

son know whether he has a vocation or not?" How would you help him?

SUGGESTIONS FOR FURTHER READING

Quentin Quesnell	*The Gospel of Christian Freedom*
Dostoevsky	"The Grand Inquisitor," a chapter from *The Brothers Karamazov*

8. Christian Choices: A Method

The Basic Principle

"The kingdom of heaven is within you," the gospel says (Lk 17:21), and the saying seems to have several levels of meaning. One of them pertains especially to our present concern, the way God ordinarily communicates with us. It amounts to this: that the will of God is found not so much in the entrails of birds as in our own entrails. It is manifest deep within, where the Spirit dwells, bearing witness with our spirit (Rm 8:16). When we come in touch with our own deepest orientation and desire, our own real interior élan, we have also found God's direction for our lives. This is the fundamental principle around which the discernment process pivots.

Suppose someone is trying to know whether he or she is called to religious life or priesthood. Where will the answer be? Not outside, but deep within. Conversations with other people will help. The steps of a formula for discernment will be of some use. Prayer will offer some guidance. But ultimately the answer is found inside the person. It is a pervasive feeling which says: "This is right for me. This fits. This is what I want to do." People who refuse to look at the possibility of a religious vocation will, if they are called, be unable to put the thought aside peacefully, precisely because it belongs to them. This is illustrated in the case of Jeremiah, the prophet, who found it difficult to be a prophet and would sometimes choose not to speak God's word.

> If I say, "I will not mention him, or speak anymore in his name," there is in my heart, as it were, a burning fire shut up in my bones, and I am weary with holding it in, and I cannot (Jer 20:9).

God's purpose for us is found deep within ourselves, in the place where we find our own profound life-orientation or destiny. What God wants for us, and what we are, are consistent with each other. The seeds of his purpose are planted within us, and from within, in interaction with an environment that is also in his hands, they would grow toward the fullness of our possibilities.

The profound psychological researches of Carl Jung are epitomized in the conclusion that the main task of life for us is "individuation," or becoming the unique individual each of us is. It is a task and a responsibility; it takes a lifetime, and can be very demanding at times. But we evade it at our peril. For Jung, it involves, among other things, listening to all the parts of the self, the rational as well as the feeling components, the conscious as well as the unconscious, which last speaks to us in dreams and other ways. All must be respected and integrated into our total unique selfhood. We have plenty of resistances to this task of becoming our own selves, not a partial self and not someone else; but we ignore our destiny at the risk of our own self-destruction. For it is impossible to be whole or to be at peace until we find and follow our own path.

Jung's analysis dovetails with and buttresses the view of spiritual discernment we are presenting. Jung looks within, particularly into the deeper recesses of the self, to find the direction of one's life, the clues to one's authentic unfolding. Jung believes in God. But he looks mainly within the personality to find God's leadings. His keen interest in dreams, as an important avenue of communication from still unconscious parts of the personality, bears a striking likeness to the Bible's interest in dreams, in both Old and New Testaments, as an important avenue of communication from God. Jung's life was filled with direction-giving dreams, particularly at critical junctures, and his own sense of vocation and personal destiny were as strong as those of any person who has spoken in more traditional religious categories.

Our interest here is not precisely in dreams, but in making contact with our profound life-orientation as revealed in what we most deeply want. In quest of that, one of the essential steps is distinguishing wants from shoulds.

Wants are mine; shoulds are someone else's. Someone else's shoulds, whether they be my parents', the church's, my culture's, or my peer group's, can be so deeply ingested by me that they almost seem to be my own. Yet often they are not, and usually they get separated out when they are tested by various pressures. With a want, the case is different. It comes not from outside, but from inside. I can really own it as mine. People can push up against it, circumstances may put it severely to the test, living it may be attended with great difficulty, but I persevere because I am motivated by something I really want. An example would be the excavations of Howard Carter in quest of King Tutankamen's tomb. For six years his efforts yielded nothing, yet year after year he was at the job. It takes more than somebody else's idea or somebody else's money to keep a person at a task like that. He wanted something.

Not only can wants be distinguished from shoulds. There is a clear distinction between "I want" and "I would like," and this has to be understood too before we can take our wants seriously. There are many things I would like. I would like to be married to a younger woman—at least for a few days. Do I really want it? No. I would like to have a Ph.D. Do I really want it? No. I would like to be more active in justice concerns. Do I really want it? No. Many such things are mere velleities, whims, fancies. They are things I talk about but never do anything about, which shows that I do not want them very much. I would like to quit smoking or lose weight. This same superficial level of wanting is expressed also in "I feel like." I feel like punching you in the nose. I feel like shoplifting a desirable item from a store. I feel like walking out on home and family. When we speak of locating our deepest level of wanting in our quest of God's purposes for us, we are not talking about whimsical wishes or passing feelings of this sort. We are speaking of something serious, a wanting which engages our personhood. We mean wholehearted wanting.

The name of St. Ignatius Loyola is usually linked with the practice of discernment in the church, because he made some very important contributions to it. It is interesting in our present context to notice how he approaches a retreat, in which people usually make important life-decisions. He does not lay out a detailed program for the living out of one's life. He merely says that its basic orientation should be toward God. He nowhere asserts the proposition that the harder thing is the better thing in the Christian life. And when he presents basic principles to the director of the retreat, he admonishes him or her not to persuade the retreatant to any particular course, even to a commendable course such as a stricter observance of poverty or entering religious life. He counsels the director rather to remain in equilibrium, open to any possibility, allowing God to deal directly with the retreatant without interference. In other words, he does not know where a person should come out. The director goes into the dialogue with no preplan. He or she wishes merely to facilitate the retreatant's communion with God, so that God's leading might be felt. Ignatius eschews outside influences in favor of a person's openness to the stirrings deep within, where God's Spirit dwells. He has the retreatant pay close attention to his or her own feelings.

The spiritual director, therefore, whether inside or outside a retreat, is doing something at once spiritual and psychological. The goal is to help a person get in touch with his or her own deepest wanting, on the conviction that being authentically oneself and being the person God wants one to be are one and the same. The director is trying to help a person separate out genuine deep wanting both from extrinsic shoulds and from trivial passing fancies, and to encourage a person to move confidently in the direction of his or her own deep wanting, as the surest index he or she has of God's purpose.

This brings psychology and spirituality together also on the question of personal growth. Growth is ownership of one's own personhood, movement in the direction of being ever more genuinely oneself. Growth is integration of all the elements of personality, emotional and rational, unconscious and conscious, in such a way that a person can be one and wholehearted in the execution of the deepest life-élan. Wholehearted wanting is the only sound basis of motivation. Growth before God as well as among one's fellow human be-ings is growth in autonomy, the acceptance of one's freedom as gift, possibility, and responsibility. To the question: "God, what is your will for me?" the answer is understood to be: "I want you to be your-self. I leave the details of that up to you."

The Ignatian Discernment Framework

The Ignatian method for discerning God's will, or making choices in the Lord, involves three steps. Examining them in some detail at this juncture will help us contextualize the points we have seen so far, and give them confirmation from a different perspective.

1.   Praying for Freedom and Guidance

The first step in the procedure is prayer. One prays for two things: indifference and guidance. Indifference means freedom from undue influence, a kind of psychic equilibrium in which one can hear God's word above all other voices. This is an indispensable condi-tion, for if one already knows how one is finally going to choose, it is like rigging an election. One might as well not bother going through the process at all. Of course, in many matters, one will start with a strong personal preference. What one is then praying for is freedom with respect to this preference, so that it will not determine the final choice. The other part of one's prayer is for guidance, guid-ance in the judgments one makes, so that they will be informed by Christian values and based on an accurate assessment of one's situ-ation and possibilities. What is envisioned here is not just a single prayer for these two graces, but prayer all through the period of one's discernment. For Ignatius, the indispensable condition for making a proper discernment is that the fundamental orientation of life be right, i.e., that it be really directed toward God, so that one desires nothing more earnestly than to live in the Lord. The kind of prayer we are describing here strengthens this sort of orientation, asking as it does precisely for freedom and for guidance toward the best possible decision. It is important to be steeped in such prayer. In the *Spiritual Exercises,* for instance, the discernment process about the specifics of one's following of Christ does not begin until well into the retreat, in the midst of meditations and contemplations on the life of Christ.

2. Assessing the Data

The second step in the discernment process is an open assessment of the facts of the case. If I am contemplating moving from one location to another, from one job to another, from one way of life to another, I take inventory of what losses would be entailed and what gains. I look honestly at all the factors in the picture—why I want to make this choice, how it would affect me, how it would affect others, how it might affect my relationship with God.

In trying to sort out the jumble of my thoughts and feelings, a couple of devices can be quite helpful. The first is to talk the issues through with another person. This is where the Christian helper comes in, to serve not in the capacity of judge, but simply as reflector, not giving advice, but merely attending, summarizing, clarifying. The helper might also feed back the feelings he or she hears behind the words.

It is important that this role be clear and properly played. The helper is an active listener and companion in the search. He or she is not the final decider, the advice-giver, or the subtle persuader. These misguided playings of the part are harder to avoid than might appear. One has to be aware of one's biases. Many priests and religious have gone to psychological counselors with personal problems, and found themselves advised to leave their way of life, though in their minds this was hardly the issue. The counselor had a bias against celibacy. Many married couples caught in patterns destructive of themselves and their children, trying to assess themselves honestly before a priest or minister, have met with the unshakable judgment that even thinking of separation or divorce was a violation of God's will. This is a bias too. Priests and religious have gone to superiors and spiritual directors with a deep and persistent doubt about the suitability of their way of life for themselves, and have felt that they were not heard, but rather that their difficulties were glossed over and answered with a spiritual pep talk. These biases in the helper are no assist to honest inquiry and balanced assessment, or to personal responsibility either. None of us is free of all bias. But we can be aware of what our biases are, state them, and allow them to be challenged.

The process of getting out the facts involves not only all that is "statistical," the relevant history, and everything pertaining to idea and principle, but the deeper feelings involved as well. For, as we have seen, feelings are very important indicators of how one actually is in a situation and of how God might be moving one from within. Particularly in dealing with an idealistic person, allowing and positively assisting the real feelings to surface, feelings sometimes suppressed because they are out of harmony with "oughts" and "shoulds," is a vital part of the process. These feelings deserve as careful a hearing as the most sacrosanct of the principles of the person's life-philosophy.

St. Ignatius suggests a couple of other instruments for helping a person with this assessment of an issue requiring choice. One is to use paper and pencil and make a list of the pros and cons that go with each of the alternatives. The purpose is simply objectification. Things usually become clearer if we can somehow get them out of our insides and see them in the light of day. This method of objectification on paper can be used in the absence of someone to bounce things off of, or in conjunction with such a helper, in preparation for the conversation. In either case, part of the genius of the pro-and-con approach is to try to think prayerfully and seriously on one side at a time, i.e., not just to consider alternatives, but to consider them separately and at length. One first thinks of all the reasons *against* a particular course of action, and tries living for a while hypothetically in that choice, to see what it feels like. Only then does one turn to thinking of all the reasons *for* the course of action, and again tries living uninterruptedly for a while hypothetically in that choice, to see what that feels like. This can be quite a help to clarification, more helpful usually than simply vacillating back and forth haphazardly.

Ignatius also suggests some simple exercises to clarify perspectives. He invites us to imagine ourselves on our deathbeds and to ask what we will then wish we had chosen. This may sound as if it were meant to inspire fear in the face of an impending judgment. Its point is rather to broaden perspective, to help me look up from the matter which immediately occupies me to the panorama of my whole life and what I want it to be. Ignatius also suggests imagining some other person coming to us with the very dilemma we have. How do we think that person should choose? These two devices help the objectification process by offering some distance.

3. Seeking Confirmation in Peace

The third step in the discernment process is the receiving of confirmation of our choice from God. This confirmation comes in the form of his peace. Peace may be unmistakably spiritual and deeply felt. Or it may be just a simple but sure sense that our choice is right. The choice falls into place; it fits. It puts or leaves us in harmony with ourselves.

It is important to distinguish this feeling of rightness from the peace which comes from the mere fact of making a decision, so that one is no longer on the fence. This is some relief, but not in itself the peace we mean. Neither is the feeling of relief which comes from choosing to escape from a difficult situation, though that too is immediately comfortable. We are speaking of a peace which is identical with a sense of rightness or of being in harmony with oneself.

Even at that, peace is rarely pure and untrammeled. The choice we make is rarely without its difficulties, and sometimes its difficulties are great. The prospect of these difficulties mars our peace somewhat. We may be choosing to accept a position of major responsibility in a religious or social institution, to stick with a trying marital or religious commitment, to confront unjust social structures whose reprisals are swift and terrible, to renounce a position or a relationship which has become dear, to leave the security of our present station for terrain yet untracked. There is no way in our life-choices to make all the pluses come out on one side of the matter and all the minuses on the other. Our peace will not be perfect if we put mother in a nursing home; nor will it be perfect if we keep her. In this as in most of life's ambiguities, we are usually left with some values which we could not honor, some things to continue to struggle with, some things to endure. We make a point of this here because some presentations of discernment sound as if some unimaginable peace floods our hearts after a good discernment, so that we wonder how we could ever have wondered in the first place. It is not usually so. More commonly, when we choose in the Lord we simply feel basically right about it, and, in that sense, essentially at peace. This is the indication for which we are watching.

What we are trying to describe here can be illustrated by the case of Jesus in the garden, after his struggle, at the point where he has resolved to go through with his passion. He is presumably at peace in the sense sketched above, even though what he faces is terribly disturbing and saddening. It also seems safe to say that he is choosing to do what he most deeply wants to do, even though there are more superficial levels in himself which do not want passion and death at all. He feels called to do this, and he is at one with himself in doing it. In Luke's account, an angel has come to comfort him in his choice, i.e., to strengthen him in it. "I have a baptism to be baptized with; and how I am constrained until it is accomplished!" (Lk 12:50). "I lay down my life for my sheep" (Jn 10:15). He wants to do it. He has come to peace.

Our review of the Ignatian discernment process shows that St. Ignatius and Carl Jung are presenting the same fundamental idea in different ways. For Ignatius, a choice in harmony with God's will brings peace; a choice out of harmony with God's will brings perturbation. For Jung, a choice in harmony with our true self brings peace and wholeness; a choice out of harmony with our true self produces anxiety and neurotic symptoms—headaches, ulcers, depression, guilt. Whether psychologically or spiritually considered, the situation is the same. We must be ourselves. But the self we must be is the self we most deeply want to be. Desire and destiny meet, our deepest wanting and God's purpose for us. The answer is to be sought within. Peace tells us we have found it.

The Role of the Helper

Let us bring our discussion to a close by summing up the kinds of assistance the Christian helper can offer someone who wants to make a choice or decision in the Lord. The first is to share the method, the three steps in a discernment process. The second is to function within it, as listener, reflector, asker of questions, fellow explorer, occasion for objectification. The key function here is to help people find the center of themselves, to get in touch with their deepest wanting, and to separate this out from "I should," "I would like," and "I feel like," since wholehearted wanting is the only sound basis of motivation. The third is to share a theology of God's will or purpose for us, and the meaning of the gift of freedom God gives us, so that the person is not frantically trying to find the preplan or exact course of action God has eternally decreed. In accordance with this, it is helpful to let the person know that certitude is hard to come by. The larger issues of life are complex, with important values on both sides of any choice we make, and God does not usually give clear directions. We are left largely to our wits, our instincts, our strongest surmise. Thomas More put it well in *A Man for All Seasons:*

> "God made the angels to show him splendor—as he made animals for innocence and plants for their simplicity. But Man he made to serve him wittily, in the tangle of his mind."

We can trust God to accept and bless any choice we make after we have done all we reasonably can to make that choice well. Lastly, the helper can warn a person not to try a process of discernment on every choice of his or her life. It is cumbersome, and too much of it could drive a person crazy. Its usefulness is its applicability to the larger and more far-reaching choices, not to all the little decisions of every day. The big ones take and deserve time. The lesser ones fall into place in a harmonious way if our sights are set on the Lord in an habitual attitude of life.

Where God's will is concerned, the analogy of good parents dealing with their children is illuminating. If parents love their children, they want life for them in the fullest possible measure. They want them to be mature, balanced, happy, free. They hope they will be discriminating, loving, bent on true value. They have not preconceived in much detail what will be good for their children. This they leave to the children themselves. Forming them as best they can, especially in their earlier years, they gradually give them more and more autonomy, allowing their choices to unfold naturally out of the developing sense of self.

We have indicated the reasons for thinking it is much the same between God and ourselves. He has not preconceived the pattern of our lives in much detail. He loves us and wants life for us; and, like good parents, he is content to give us our heads and let our choices naturally unfold out of our developing selfhood. Discernment, then, is not a magical formula for ferreting out the hidden plan, but a procedure for using our best human resources, in the context of prayerfulness and a life-orientation toward God, to frame and make those choices which seem most consonant with our selfhood and God's overarching purpose revealed in Christ.

QUESTIONS FOR REFLECTION AND DISCUSSION

1. What are the three steps in the Ignatian method for making a good choice?

2. In what ways can the Christian helper assist someone in the making of a good choice?

3. What are some of the pitfalls the helper must be careful to avoid in this particular function?

4. Is there any way one can know with certainty that one's choice has been made in the Lord?

5. Is one's deepest wanting really a reliable criterion in the search for God's will? How is it different from selfishness?

6. What, if anything, does Carl Jung have to contribute to the discussion of choosing in the Lord?

7. What practical tips does St. Ignatius offer those in the reflective or data-gathering stage of a discernment process?

SUGGESTIONS FOR FURTHER READING

John English	*Spiritual Freedom*
Carl Jung	*Memories, Dreams and Reflections*
Ignatius Loyola	*The Spiritual Exercises,* especially "Annotations," "The Election," "Rules for Discernment of Spirits"
Robert Mellert	*What is Process Theology?*

9. Pitfalls

Christian helping has its hazards. There are things we can do to ourselves as well as to others that are not in the best interest of either. Many of them are quite subtle, and we are scarcely aware that we do them. Let us take a look at some of the main ones.

Too Directive

One of the subtle temptations of the helper is to become parent to the person who comes, and treat him or her as child. The helper listens a little bit, and then takes charge. One can seize the role of teacher, and explain all kinds of things to the other. One can become cheerleader, and give pep talks. One can act as God, and tell the other how to live his or her life. One can assume the posture of judge, and put strictures on what the other can say or think or feel or do. In short, one can become much too talkative and loom way too large. It is no longer the other person's concerns which constitute the agenda, but the opinions, stories, exhortations, and directions of the helper. Those seeking help have the sense of pushing buttons and getting speeches, putting quarters in a record player and getting songs, dialing a saint and getting a message from the Lord. So they leave not only bearing the burden they came with, but other baggage besides. They have the distressing feeling that they have not been heard—or helped.

People have an uncanny capacity to heal themselves. What is true of the body is true of psyche and spirit as well. The body, when it suffers injury or disease, has a self-healing mechanism which gradually brings restoration. Psyche and spirit work to restore themselves in a similar way. C. G. Jung is emphatic in maintaining that the deepest tendency of the human psyche is to integrate the diverse elements of the personality and experience into wholeness and health. The helper needs to rely on this psychic resourcefulness of the other, and to make an ally of it. People can usually solve their own problems or find the inner strength to bear the burdens they must bear, if we but let them talk things through. To talk out is to objectify, and to objectify is to see in a new way. The helper is a welcoming occasion for the objectification of experience, so that the other person, now in better possession of what had been a jumble inside, can take what measures suggest themselves.

People seeking help sometimes begin the conversation by saying they do not know where to begin. Exactly. This is why they have come. Tell them to begin in the middle, and by the time they finish they will usually know where the beginning, middle, and end are. They will also have caught what is foolish in their utterances without having it pointed out, spotted relations they had not seen before, separated the wheat from the chaff, and gained insight into themselves. It might take a bit of feedback to bring them to these things—a clarifying question, a tentative summary. But they can do most of the work, and need to do most of the work themselves. It is needless, then, and positively obstructive, for the helper to become too directive, too judgmental, too authoritative.

Too Talkative

This pitfall is related to the last, but there are many more kinds of talkativeness than just overdirectiveness. The helper sometimes asks too many questions. The other is thus subtly diverted from what he or she has really come to say. The helper is trying to find out what that actually is but may be leading away from it without realizing it. It is better, as far as possible, just to let the account run, letting the pieces fall in place on their own terms. One's questions too easily proceed from needless curiosity, from one's own sense of order, from uncomfortableness with a silence, from the desire to pursue an hypothesis and reach an analysis. People frequently prefer just to be allowed to talk, without being pumped too much for clarification or details until they have gotten the whole story out. Then there may be a place for some questions, to supply genuinely important elements which have been omitted, or to prompt some reflection back over what has been said. Again, the value of simply attending to and empathizing with someone who wants to talk can hardly be overstressed.

Some helpers are tempted to chime in too much with their own experience. The person no sooner begins to talk about something than they say, "Oh, yes, I know exactly what you mean." Or, "You think *that's* bad. Let me tell you about the time. . . ." And they launch into their own experience. The floor is finally regained by the person seeking help, but he or she is in possession only long enough to provide the helper with another stimulus. In the end the person seeking help knows quite a bit more about the helper than the helper knows about the person seeking help.

It is good to show such persons that we are in tune, that we understand what they are going through, that they are not the only person in the world with this problem. But the process goes amuck when the spotlight shifts to the helper. There are doubtless times when sharing a personal experience can be invaluable to someone. But those times should be chosen sparingly and with discretion, and experience should be so shared that it leads back to the other person's experience. What is most important in the healing process is that the troubled person feel heard, understood, and accepted. Listening to parallel stories is a poor substitute for that vital happening. The helper needs to beware here of the need to seem important, interesting, or widely experienced.

Flattered

Another pitfall is allowing one's own needs to dominate the relationship. This happens when one needs to be a helper to feel a sense of worth. One goes out and seeks counselees, keeps count of them, rejoices in any increment, competes with other helpers, moves to increase the frequency of meetings, needs expressions of appreciation and affection from those being helped, takes it personally if someone indicates a desire to terminate or transfer or confides in anyone else simultaneously.

The portrait is perhaps somewhat overdrawn, but there is an unfreedom at work here which vitiates the helping relationship. Whenever such a relationship is initiated or maintained for the sake of the helper rather than for the sake of the person supposedly in need of help, the air waves are too trammeled for genuinely constructive communication. Again, all is confusion, and the relationship works to foster dependency rather than autonomy and growth. There is a parallel here with parents who are emotionally overinvested in their children. Their own marital relationship is poor (or, in the case of single parents, non-existent), and/or they have no satisfying peer relationships or outside activities. So they bind their children to themselves, and will not let them go. None of us is completely free of the kind of needs or emotional unfreedoms here described. Perhaps we never will be. But in the interest of those we would help, we need to do battle with them.

Enmeshed

Some helpers succumb to the temptation to become too involved with others, and allow the problems of others to wreck their own peace and happiness. They carry the problems of all the people they are trying to help, and sometimes, by attraction, of the world as well. They catch the disease they want to cure. There is a delicate balance here. A genuine involvement with the person in need is crucial to the fruitfulness of the relationship. The cold, calculating, distant listener is scarcely a help to the troubled human being. Yet a certain emotional distance from the problems of others is vital to our own equanimity and our usefulness to them. It is also essential to our longer-range survival as helpers. To be concerned, to feel for others, to wonder how they are doing in the intervals between conversations, to pray for them—all these are in order. But if one cannot relax, sleep, or celebrate, if one dare not go out for a good time, if one loses the capacity for laughter because this person has been jilted in love, that person is dying, or someone else is going through the dark night of the soul, one is killing oneself to no avail. For what does it avail these suffering others? In the words of Shakespeare, "It not enriches them, and makes me poor indeed" (*Othello,* III, 3).

The example of Jesus is instructive here. He bore our griefs and carried our sorrows (Is 53:4). He felt compassion for the multitudes because they were harassed and helpless like sheep without a shepherd (Mt 9:36). Yet there are two unforgettable New Testament images of him. One is of Jesus at table with tax collectors and sinners, in such a style as to have earned him the reputation of being "a glutton and a drunkard" (Lk 7:34). The other is of Jesus in the midst of the storm, asleep in the stern on a cushion (Mk 4:38). In the psalms and in the wisdom literature, sleep is a mark of the just, who rest secure because of their trust in God and the rightness of their relationship with him. Jesus can sleep even in the midst of the storm. His capacity both for celebration and for serenity in the midst of a troubled world is grounded in his unshakable trust in God.

Freedom from this particular affliction comes, then, from some combination of enough to occupy one's time and energy, insight into the fruitlessness of my anxiety for the other person's relief, and trust in the God of Abraham, Isaac, and Jacob.

Discouraged

Then there is the pitfall of being troubled because one feels that what one does is never enough. One listens with care, but cannot take grief away. One hears heart-rending stories, offers support, makes suggestions, even sees progress sometimes. Yet progress is slow, the awful struggle with weakness and pain continues, and there is backward as well as forward movement. What good is one really doing? It is never enough. The incidence of suicide is high among those engaged in the helping professions. Helpers are privy to so much pain, and powerless to take most of it away.

Part of the antidote to the helper's blues is remembering the positive side of the picture. A person making slow progress might, without our help, be making no progress at all, or even be getting worse. The person who shares with us a burden we cannot remove might otherwise have no one with whom even to share it. For some people, we are the lifeline, the last bastion against despair, the single oasis in all a barren terrain, no matter how small our apparent ministry. There are, of course, real limits to what one can do. But something is better than nothing. The other part of the antidote is prayer. We rely on God to supply what we lack, to work through our inadequacy, to follow the person those ways we cannot. By recourse to prayer the Christian helper, though a mere earthen vessel, becomes a blessing to the other, and the other to him or her.

Inhibiting

These last couple of items have been things we do to ourselves. There is another obstacle we can put in the way of others, and that is to hinder their free communication by the narrowness and rigidity of our presuppositions. A good helper is maximally permissive, in the sense that he or she gives the other person the freedom to say anything at all. This is liberation, because what the other is feeling may be anger at God, hostility at you, erotic desire for you or someone else, hatred of self, or a sense of the absurdity of all living. What the other is thinking may challenge your most cherished convictions. A priest who had been doing psychotherapy and spiritual direction for years once remarked to me that if you are really going to listen to someone else, you have to be prepared to have all your assumptions called into question. This is not the most comfortable of experiences. You may be convinced that homosexual expression is an unnatural activity engaged in only by the despicable, and find yourself listening to a man or woman you respect and love very much telling you that he or she does it and finds it life-giving. You may be convinced that premarital sex is always out of place and wreaks destruction on those who indulge in it, yet find yourself listening to a man and woman of integrity and good judgment telling you that they engage in it and judge it good. You may be convinced that an ordained person or a man or woman with religious vows is strictly obliged to bear out those commitments till death, yet find yourself listening to someone who is being destroyed by such a commitment and feels that he or she is being led by God to a different way of life. The same is possible in the case of a validly contracted Christian marriage. So you are faced with a choice. Either you bend people to fit your categories of understanding, denying their experience or their honesty and perhaps forcing them to make a choice not in their best interest; or you allow your assumptions to be called into question and your understanding to be revised, at least provisionally, by the testimony of their experience. People in official positions in the church are particularly hard pressed in these situations if they see themselves mainly as guardians of unquestionable laws and traditions.

There are subtler ways to inhibit honest self-exploration and communication. Some helpers, more likely men, are made very uncomfortable by tears. Others try to quell or cover any appearance of anger in the person seeking help. Some are quick to move in and refute expressions of discouragement or the calling in question of life and God. Others become perceptibly uncomfortable if sexual matters are brought up. Some change the subject as soon as someone discloses warm positive feelings for them, or become defensive at the expression of negative feelings, without examining their grounds. All this activity is inhibiting, and blocks the other person's process. People are often ashamed enough of their feelings, without the need of having their shame reinforced. Their healing lies in getting the feelings out into the open, and having them accepted as legitimate, not in their being more firmly repressed. Here the cardinal principle of Transactional Analysis is applicable: "Feelings are neither good nor bad; they just are." We are passive to our feelings, and simply find them inside. Some we wish we did not have—hatred of parents, fear of peers, sexual desire in the wrong circumstances, jealousy, hurt, guilt, grudges. Yet we seem unable to shake them off. Healing lies in the direction of coming to comfortableness with the feelings which we and others actually have, realizing that it is not so strange to have them, and knowing that we can act on them or not as we choose. Feelings are prior to freedom, and so are not a matter of moral concern. They do not necessarily determine our choices, which are where freedom and responsibility lie. Coming to this kind of comfortableness with one's feelings depends often on being able to tell them to someone else and see them understood and accepted. That not only makes them more acceptable to us; it often works to rob unwanted feelings of their power. They thrive in hiddenness more than they do in revelation. This is why it is such a disservice to someone to inhibit his or her disclosure of feelings, especially the embarrassing and painful ones. To be a good helper is to be an old shoe, very permissive in this area, and none the worse for wear.

Too directive, too talkative, flattered, enmeshed, discouraged, inhibiting. There are probably other snares as well. The work goes on though we are snared, but these things do hurt it, or us. They happen when we lose perspective on our role.

QUESTIONS FOR REFLECTION AND DISCUSSION

1. Can a helper be too directive? How? Might a helper also be too non-directive?

2. How can pursuing a line of questioning work against the helping process?

3. What guidelines should govern the sharing of personal experiences in the helping relationship?

4. How can the helper avoid getting weighed down by, or too involved in, the problems of the people he or she is helping?

5. I am a helper, generally pretty good at it, judging by folks' feedback. But I am uncomfortable with one or other of:
   a. people who talk about sex
   b. people who cry
   c. people who warm up to me too much
   d. people who ask me why God allows so much misery
   e. people who question church teaching
   f. people who are angry
   g. people who are depressed time after time.
   What should I do?

6. What are the main pitfalls in helping relationships for you?

10. Preparing Oneself

We have treated some of the basic operations of the Christian helper or spiritual director, and indicated some of the demands of that role. Two questions rather naturally present themselves: Am I called to serve in such a capacity? If so, how can I prepare myself more adequately to do it? Let us address these questions now.

Am I Cut Out for This?

Spiritual directors, and this is the term we will use in the present chapter, are born, not made. Spiritual direction is a charism or gift of God, not a skill humanly acquired. To some it is given, to others not. Those who do not have it may be Christians of the highest quality, but they do not have this particular gift. Those who do have it may go through a significant portion of their lives before discovering that they have it. In any case, it is a gift, some combination of "discernment," "wisdom," and "healing" in Paul's list of the service gifts of the Spirit (1 Cor 12:4–11). One's skills in the area of spiritual direction can certainly be developed, and it is important that they be, but what is required above all is something foundational—a certain kind of person or a certain set of personal qualities. Given these, the edifice can be built. Without them, years of schooling do not produce the desired product. The same thing can be observed in the professional area of psychotherapy. There are plenty of degreed people around, but not a few of them turn in a poor performance. At the same time, ironically, some people who have not had the training and lack the credentials prove to have uncanny insight into the troubled and to be of great assistance to them.

How then do I know whether I have the gift or not? For one thing, people usually tell me. They might tell me directly, might even encourage me to get further training and work full-time in some helping capacity. More often, they tell me indirectly, by coming to me for help. If I am the sort of person people naturally confide in or look to for advice when they are trying to cope with difficult situations, this is a pretty good sign that I am equipped for this sort of thing. It is the best testimony of all. If I have a capacity for close and deep friendships, and in my life with people get habitually into the deeper realms of sharing and searching together, this is a promising sign. If people seem to respect me as having some insight or wisdom or spiritual acumen, if they show an inclination to trust me and tell me their stories, I have a pretty good indication that I have the foundational gifts of the spiritual director.

There is another sign too. I really want to be a spiritual director. I am interested in it and feel attracted to it. When I check my motives, I do not find them to be a need to be needed or to be looked up to and thought wise or spiritual, but rather just a desire to be helpful to people who want to grow in the Christian life and a sense that God has given me some ability to do that. Any vocation we can think of is indicated by some combination of these two factors: a desire within myself to do it, and confirmations from persons and circumstances outside myself.

Building on the Foundations

Picking up a thread from an earlier chapter, we note first that seriousness about one's own growth is the first requirement. I will not ask others to do what I do not take the trouble to do myself. Nor will I deal in realms in which I have no experience. I resolve to try to understand myself, to face myself, and to grow. I will be reflective and prayerful. I will endeavor to make the important choices of my life in the Lord. I will be open to the truth about myself and about the meaning of life, wherever I hear that truth spoken. I will strive to live the truth I see.

Next, I will allow myself to be helped. I will seek spiritual direction. One can learn a lot from the other side of the desk, whether it be teaching or counseling that one observes. Being directed by someone else acquaints one at first hand with the sorts of things that come up and the ways they are dealt with. I will have opportunity to notice both what helps and what hinders, and can reflect on precisely what it is that I want a helper to do for me. I will have direct experience of the relative importance and impact of such factors in the director as warmth, wisdom, listening, asking questions, giving advice, sharing personal experience, praying together. This will help me make my own decisions as director about the best proportions and usage of these things.

If it is for the giving of individually directed retreats that I wish to prepare myself, then it is very helpful to make several of them, and to make them with various directors, in order to observe the variety of approaches to the same task, again taking account of what helps and what hinders. The same holds true for ongoing spiritual direction outside the retreat situation. The ideal background is to have been directed over the years by several people. Not only will this acquaint me with differing approaches. It will also show me how my needs as directee change over time, how varied are the life-situations in which I seek direction, and how subtly different are the ways God deals with me in the retreat situation and in day-to-day living outside times of retreat.

All that has been said so far pertains to experience, the best teacher. What follows pertains more to schooling.

Important Areas of Knowledge

It is indispensable to the spiritual director to be familiar with scripture. Scripture is the inspired word of God, the basic constitution of the Christian life, the ultimate norm for the path any Christian treads. Acquaintance and familiarity with it equips one with the basic theology out of which one works—who God is, who Jesus is, what the church is, what the sacraments mean, how prayer functions in the Christian life, what the moral bases of Christian choice are, what the criteria are for distinguishing the spirits by which we are moved. Besides being a theological resource, scripture is the privileged source of prayer. The director should know how to pray from scripture and how to teach others to do so, as this is one of the most frequently made requests.

Finally, familiarity with scripture, and particularly with where things are in scripture, puts one in a good position to be able to suggest passages to people according to their needs. In a retreat or ongoing spiritual direction situation, it may become evident that someone particularly needs to develop faith, or trust in God, or sorrow for sin, or a sense of God's mercy, or personal responsibility, or a spirit of prayerfulness. One may be involved in life-situations for which scripture supplies rich paradigms. It is very advantageous to be able to put one's finger on passages which speak to these needs. What is called for in all this is not that the spiritual director be a scripture scholar. But the more acquaintance one has, the better equipped one is. One can take advantage of course or workshop opportunities, and be oneself an habitual reader of scripture. Where reading is concerned, it can be made much more instructive by the use of some commentary, at least to the extent of reading an introduction to the scripture one has chosen, the better to understand its historical context, structure, and significant theological themes.

Next in the line of academic preparations is the study of theology. Again, one need not be a professional theologian to be a spiritual director, but theology helps. Consciously or unconsciously, one works out of a set of theological assumptions and principles. In dealing with those who wish to grow, the more one knows especially of moral and spiritual theology, and of how the church and the Christian life are understood today in the light both of the tradition and of contemporary knowledge and insight, the richer will be the context out of which one works. To be a theologian, or even a scripture scholar, is by no means to be a spiritual director. On the other hand, a spiritual director trying to operate without much scripture or theology is poor in resources, and possibly even seriously misguided in theoretical framework.

If it is retreat work one wishes to do, one needs some theoretical knowledge of the retreat framework within which one intends to work. If, for instance, one chooses to work out of the *Spiritual Exercises* of St. Ignatius, then some study of the *Exercises* is necessary over and above the experience of making them. To direct individuals in an Ignatian retreat, one needs a conceptual grasp of the dynamic of the *Exercises*—overall, week by week, and in particular meditations or contemplations. Not everyone who is able to speak a native language can teach it well, nor can every doctor who practices surgery skillfully impart that skill to others. What is needed is reflex knowledge, a conceptual grasp of the procedures one follows in practice by unconscious instinct. The best time for such reflection and explicitation where retreat-giving is concerned is shortly after actually making a retreat. There are several fine training programs now available which offer such a sequence. The prospective director first makes the *Exercises,* then studies their structure and dynamic, and finally gives a retreat, under supervision, to someone else. The same sort of preparation would seem appropriate for work in any retreat or renewal framework.

Another important item on the list of academic needs is psychology. All helping is interpersonal, and the more one knows of the person and of the interpersonal, the better one can relate to others in a helpful way. What is needed is not something esoteric, but a basic grasp of human psychodynamics and some familiarity with interpersonal skills. Again, certain people seem to be born with these things or to have acquired them very early in life. But training is needed too. Good spiritual directors are naturally self-reflective, and have a good grasp of their own psychic life. They know how to talk with people, how to listen empathetically and perceptively, and how to express themselves clearly and appropriately. They pick up nonverbal as well as verbal communication. They can ask questions which prompt heuristic reflection, can give freedom and leave responsibility where they belong, and can help someone sort through a rambling report. They know how to clarify a confused message by checking out what they heard. They are at home in the world of feelings, their own and the other person's. They understand how to give constructive feedback. They also know when what they are dealing with goes beyond their competence, and they can refer it to someone better qualified. These are the things which are sought in the kind of psychological formation here envisaged. Course work is helpful, and workshops of various sorts are a fine supplement. Again, this is an area where reading should go on continually, as these are developing sciences. Freud and Jung are the great explorers of the unconscious, and there is a wealth of practical psychology available in Gestalt Therapy, Transactional Analysis, Psychosynthesis, and such techniques as Progoff's journaling. All of this is useful.

Finally, one will want to be schooled particularly in the area of one's specialized ministry. If it is work with youth, one will want to learn all one can about adolescent psychology and development, including faith development. If it is with religious or priests, one should know something of their histories and spiritualities, and the challenges of the present time. If it is marriage preparation or marriage counseling, there is another abundant literature for one's instruction and broadening. If it is ministry to the sick and dying, one should be familiar with what has been written in that area. The general counselor will also want to be apprised of the now commonly accepted stages of childhood development and of the newly emerging stages of adult development. Also helpful to the spiritual director is some ongoing association with others engaged in the same work, so that experience and insight, success and failure, can be shared and profited from.

This may all sound a bit overwhelming. It is an ideal sketch. It indicates the areas of experience and knowledge on which the spiritual director draws. No one can be an expert in all these domains. In particular ministries, some areas will be considerably more important than others. There is also a lifetime to work at these ideals, as both experience and theoretical knowledge gradually accumulate. It is a mistake to think that one must be fully equipped for any contingency before one begins. On this principle, no one would ever start.

On the other hand, a note of warning needs to be sounded. Christian helpers without the necessary qualifications can do great harm. Perhaps some of us have had the experience of suffering this kind of harm at the hands of others—confessors, teachers, religious formation personnel, spiritual directors, born-again Christians—and so have some sense of the danger of bending people out of shape. A little knowledge is a dangerous thing. So is bad theology, even if one has a lot of it. Even more dangerous is the lack of those personal qualities which enable one to relate in flexible and helpful ways. For the sake of those whose lives we affect, we need to let ourselves be screened by others, and to make use of supervision and consultation until we feel quite sure of ourselves. The truth may be that we are very good Christians, and gifted in many ways, yet not cut out for service in this particular role.

But some people are. And one of the ways we can foster the emergence of the qualified is to let them know about their gifts.

QUESTIONS FOR REFLECTION AND DISCUSSION

1. What are the personal gifts which indicate an aptitude for spiritual direction?

2. What background experiences prepare a person for giving good spiritual direction?

3. What are the main areas in which one needs education and training to do good spiritual direction?

4. What do you yourself most need to be better equipped for this ministry?

SUGGESTIONS FOR FURTHER READING

Gerard Egan   *The Skilled Helper*

Eugene Kennedy   *On Becoming a Counselor*

John English   *Spiritual Freedom*

Thomas Harris   *I'm OK, You're OK*

11. Typical Situations

We have been dealing in principles, looking at the theological presuppositions which constitute the framework for Christian helping relationships. It might be helpful at this point to become more concrete, and to say something about the kinds of situations which develop. What is envisioned is not strategies for dealing with adolescents, with marriage problems, with depressed persons, with those going through spiritual purifications, or with persons who are terminally ill. That would be another book, with at least as many chapters as there are types of problems. Our aim is more modest—to say something about the typical sorts of interaction that arise as one deals with persons of any age or circumstances who wish to grow in the Christian life. In the present chapter we will look at the opening interview of a spiritual direction relationship, and then deal with certain types of persons: those with very low self-regard, those who need mostly confirmation, those who have little to say, and those who never stop talking.

The Opening Interview

Let us presume that someone comes to you to open an ongoing spiritual direction relationship. What should you do in the initial conversation?

The main thing is to get some basic information, and to define subsequent procedure to some extent. While this is going on, you will also be getting a feel for the kind of person you are talking with, and he or she some sense of you.

After chatting a little bit just to establish a basic comfortableness, you might ask the person what he or she wants out of spiritual direction. Expectations are important for all that follows, and it is crucial to know what the person seeks and to respond to it. Your response may be that you cannot meet that expectation, but that you can perhaps mutually agree on another. More commonly, the person's hopes are quite reasonable and fitting, and are easily agreed to. It is just a question of finding out whether people want help on a pressing problem right now, whether they just want to walk with you for some time on their spiritual journey, or whether they wish to pursue growth in one or other particular area of felt need. This basic information gives the project some focus.

It is good in the first conversation also to make some agreements about frequency and length of the meetings to follow, and about procedure. On frequency, there is no set norm. What is agreed upon should be proportionate to the situation. If there is a pressing issue right now, weekly meetings may be required. If it is an ongoing relationship directed in a general way toward Christian growth, every four weeks may be sufficient, though a person or director may prefer to get together a little more frequently, perhaps every two or three weeks. As far as length of time is concerned, an hour seems to be a pretty generally accepted norm in all the helping professions. The hour need not always be filled, but it serves usefully as an outer limit. Knowing that there is just an hour to work in brings both persons to the point. There is a law which states that a task tends to take about as much time as you have for it.

As far as procedure is concerned, it helps to clarify who is going to take the lead. Is the person coming for help supposed to determine the agenda each time, or should he or she just come and expect the helper to take over? The former arrangement seems preferable. The person seeking help will then give some forethought to the sessions, and open with whatever is uppermost in mind, which is probably what most needs to be dealt with. Some people like to begin just by making a review of the period since the last conversation. Most people can do one or other of these without any difficulty. But there are others who genuinely want spiritual growth and therefore also spiritual direction, yet do not know what to bring up. They prefer to be asked questions, which they are quite willing to answer, but without this sort of prodding they are at a loss how to begin. If this procedure is agreed upon, then the director can occasion a sort of review each time by asking about the major areas of a person's life: prayer, work, recreation, life at home, relationships, feelings about oneself, etc. All that is needed is just some agreement about how things will generally be done. This puts both parties more at ease.

Just as it is helpful to the director to learn something about the other's expectations, so it is useful to that person to know how the director understands spiritual direction and how he or she usually goes about it. The person might wonder, for example, what sorts of things it is appropriate to talk about here, and how directive the director plans to be, or, more generally, how active in the conversation. What is the director's preferred procedure? Offering a few ideas along these lines and asking some feedback from the person seeking direction will almost certainly contribute to comfortableness.

Another important part of the first conversation is a mutual recognition that the relationship may or may not work out. If it proves not to, the person who sought help will find it far less embarrassing to pull out, or the director to suggest that he or she might wish to go to someone else.Not everyone works well with everyone else. The very best of directors sometimes encounter persons they do not understand, or like, or know how to deal with. By the same token, a person seeking help will not feel comfortable for one reason or another with a given director. The best way to deal with this possibility is to agree at the outset to try the arrangement awhile and then, after perhaps three or four conversations, to evaluate it and make a choice about continuing. Even if a mutual decision to continue comes easily, this evaluation of the state of things can lead to some constructive changes. The same sort of evaluation should be proposed again from time to time, checking particularly to see whether the person's chief expectations are being met.

If there is no particularly pressing issue the person wants to deal with in the first interview, questions might be directed to the person's history and present circumstances. Each of us being the product of the experiences and forces which have shaped us, acquaintance with these contributes greatly to understanding. Each of us is also much affected by present life-circumstances. They are the context out of which Christian growth-concerns are brought. The more the helper knows of these two areas, the more adequately he or she can respond.

All the foregoing applies in those cases where someone comes formally to initiate an ongoing helping relationship. Needless to say, the procedure is quite different when someone comes without warning, and begins to open up about some problem needing immediate attention. Then that is the matter to be dealt with, and there may be only one conversation.

At the beginning of a relationship, there is a kind of adjustment going on on both sides, a getting used to, a feeling one's way with. The person seeking help usually feels somewhat vulnerable, and some feel very vulnerable indeed. So they do a kind of testing to see whether they are safe, before they trust you with what is closest to their hearts. This is a perfectly natural human process, and should be allowed its time. In other words, the helper should not be surprised if trust does not develop right away, and should not try to push the river. A retreatant told me once that her whole retreat was ruined when, in their second conversation, her director startled her with the question, "You don't really trust me, do you?" Actually, she was not feeling any lack of trust. She was just going through the process of becoming comfortable and gradually opening up. The effect of this challenging question was to put her on edge, and make her try in all subsequent conversations to prove that she did trust her director—which got in the way of simple, straight communication. It is crucial to give people the time they need. Some who come seeking help on a particular issue, or open their lives to us in the hope of achieving personal growth, have never before talked about themselves this way with anyone.

Low Self-Esteem

In dealing with quite a number of people, it soon becomes evident that their deepest problem, deeper than the one they present, is that they do not believe they are really worthwhile. The lack of this sense of well-being dogs their steps and attaches the strongest inhibition to all they think, say, or do. They do not speak in groups, do not volunteer for activities, do not approach the stranger to make an acquaintance, because they feel so deeply they have nothing to offer. It also affects the way they pray. They are always apologizing to God. Yet, as they sit before you and talk, you find yourself moved by their obvious goodness and beauty.

Freeing people from this sort of self-imposed imprisonment is one of the greatest things a Christian helper can do for anyone. It is in the tradition of Jesus the liberator, who called Zaccheus down from his tree to lunch with him (Lk 19), publicly commended Magdalen because she loved more than her self-righteous critics (Lk 7), surprised Levi the tax collector by telling him he could be more than a tax collector (Mk 2), and made the Peter of the triple denial head of the church (Jn 21). Jesus reconstructed in people their shattered faith in themselves, and he did it simply by loving them. The result was a brand new lease on life. We can do the same thing, in the same spirit. We do it simply by responding naturally to the goodness we see in people, affirming whatever it is that we love in them, and letting them know how it really stands with them. It strikes them as all the more remarkable, since what they have come to talk about is what they do wrong and what they cannot solve and what makes them weak and needy and despicable. Their expectation is that you, the helper, having been shown these things they strive so assiduously to conceal from others, will be gentle and kind but will of course also secretly despise them. Being let into the dark places of their souls is precisely what constitutes the helper's unique healing opportunity. The Christian helper is sacrament, human incarnation of the unconditional love of God. "God was in Christ, reconciling the world to himself, not counting people's offenses against them" (2 Cor 5:19). The best way to help a person with the problem of low self-esteem and a sense of unlovableness—and such are legion—is to love them. Love them as they are. Love all the parts of them. Tell them why you love them. Love is the only thing that heals.

Needing Nothing But Confirmation

What is said here about affirmation, not artificially but naturally given, applies also to confirmation, another important part of the helper's activity. People are greatly helped by receiving some confirmation of what they are already doing. It changes nothing in their practice, but it moves them from a state of doubt to a state of reasonable assurance, and that is a big advance. To the helper, it may seem they need no help, that they know what to do in almost all situations. The helper might even begin to wonder why they come at all. The answer is that we all need reassurance. It is one thing to face a situation and come up with an approach to it, hoping it is the right approach. It is another to tell my strategy to someone else and hear that person agree that this is a good way to deal with things. The helper, of course, might sometimes not agree, which gives the other something to think about. But if the helper does agree, simply that and nothing more, the other gains confidence in his or her own judgment and more comfortableness with decisions reached. Sometimes as spiritual directors, particularly in retreat situations, we find ourselves mostly just confirming what people do as they follow their own instincts. It may not seem like much, but it is a significant service.

Very Little To Say

Sometimes we find ourselves facing a person who seems to want help, yet has very little to say. He or she comes regularly and shows good will, but is the type of person who does not talk easily or much. We find ourselves wanting more to go on, more to which we can respond. The question is how to relate constructively to such a person.

We must somehow draw him or her out. Asking questions will sometimes be enough, though it will seem to us we have to ask a great many. Allowing a silence once in a while can work too; we find out what the person does if no direction is given. There comes a moment, not too early but sometime down the road, when it is good to give a little feedback, perhaps along these lines: "You don't usually have very much to say about your experience, and I find that difficult to deal with. I am left guessing and filling in, and that is risky. Or I have to ask a lot of questions, which may not be germane. What we do here is determined almost entirely by what you bring, and if you don't bring much, I don't see how we can do much. Can you help me with this?" Then it is up to those desiring help. Maybe they will express a desire now to terminate, because they themselves do not feel much is coming of this, and feel little inclination to pursue it. Or they may indicate that they thought you were going to carry the ball more, and will change their behavior now that they know what you want. Perhaps they will simply recognize, now that you say it, that they have not been giving you enough to go on, and will make an effort to provide more. In any case, nothing is lost in giving this sort of honest feedback—provided it is not done prematurely. It is helpful to people to know how you stand with them, particularly if you tend to be generally non-directive. With people of the reticent sort, it can be helpful too to suggest aids to communication. They might keep a journal, to furnish the material for your conversations. They might express themselves and their situation better in poetry, parable, or even in painting or simple sculpture. Devices like these can sometimes really open up the deeper layers of the personality.

Too Much To Say

There are also people who are communicative to a fault. They share *everything,* without coming to any apparent point. We feel snowed, and want to break in and ask where they are going. With this type of person, it is hard to think of any device except direct feedback to stem the tide. Sometimes breaking in at some point, and asking them to return to something they just said and develop that, can work, but often such an intervention leads only to another trackless journey. Hence the need for some kind of direct feedback. Many helpers shy away from confrontation, even if it be gentle and caring confrontation. They are nice people, and do not like to hurt anyone. This needs to be looked at. The Christian ideal is not to avoid hurting people, but to avoid harming them. Peter probably did not feel very good after Jesus said to him: "Get behind me, Satan!" (Mk 8:33). The Christian ideal is to love people, and sometimes the most loving thing to do is to tell someone a painful truth. Now it is a safe bet that the way people relate to us as helpers or spiritual directors is roughly the way they relate to people in general, and that if they bore or exasperate us they probably bore and exasperate others too.

Folks who behave this way do not live very full lives. Their inter-personal relationships are few and shallow. Is it the more loving course of action, then, for the helper simply to put up with this, secretly longing for the end of the hour? Or might it be gentle but honest confrontation? Someone needs to confront this person, and most people are unwilling. We are presuming that this is not the first conversation, but the third or fourth. The garrulousness is not just initial nervousness, but a clear pattern And enough trust has developed that the helper can speak the truth and will be heard. Then it seems time to share with the person how the usual pattern of such deliverances makes us feel. We speak the truth with love (Eph 4:15). Perhaps together, then, a new strategy can be worked out for bringing the conversation around to what it ought to be. Attention may need to be called to the problem again down the road if it recurs, for such patterns do not disappear quickly.

Two Guiding Principles

Dealing with such cases as these two we have just considered calls up two guiding principles in helping relationships. The first is to pay attention to your feelings. The second is to feed back, at the appropriate time, impressions of which you have become fairly sure.

Regarding the first, feelings tell us a lot about what is going on. They often know and begin to give their signals before the mind has caught on to the dynamic. So they are invaluable aids in assessing a transaction. Why is it that I really look forward to seeing some of the folks who come to me, and feel my heart sink when others call for an appointment? Why, in the actual conversation, do I feel sometimes boredom, sometimes smoldering anger, sometimes real joy? Why do I come out of some interviews exhilarated, and out of others drained, maybe even with a headache or tight muscles in the back or neck? Do I feel seduced, distanced, used? Do I feel manipulated, burdened with impossible demands, put on a pedestal? Do I feel bored or toyed with? What I need to do is be aware of all these feelings, and then, between sessions or sometimes even during them, puzzle over these feelings to discover what it is that causes them. The feelings may tell me something about the other, or something about myself, or both. To ignore them is a waste the helper cannot afford. Our feelings have just as important things to tell us as our minds do, sometimes more important things. It may take a while to get them to come clear, but the effort is worth it for both parties. In fact, in a relationship of real trust, the helper might tell the other of the feelings before knowing where they come from, and together they can try to account for them.

The second principle is to feed back an impression that has crystalized. Here a judgment has to be made about when it should be done, and how it should be put. But it can be invaluable to another person to know how he or she comes across. We have looked at some negative impressions—that a person is too tight-lipped or too garrulous. There can be very positive ones too, for example, that someone exhibits a really impressive regard for truth, or shows remarkable honesty, or speaks of a gift of prayer that is not common. Persons may come across as very hard on themselves, as despising themselves, as having a fine sense of humor, as being affectionate, as being delightfully enthusiastic, as feeling mistrustful, as living too much in their heads, as being monotonously serious, as having always an edge of anger, as habitually locating the problem in others rather than in themselves, as having evident gifts for ministry. It aids their self-knowledge to be aware of these things. It might be helpful also to explore the roots of these things and their scope. That is why it is good not only to perceive these things but also to share them, at the right time and in the right way. It should be done tentatively, offered just as an impression, inviting some kind of affirmative or negative response. This is sometimes easy to do, sometimes difficult. In either case, it is a gift to the other.

QUESTIONS FOR REFLECTION AND DISCUSSION

1. What are the main objectives in the opening interview?

2. What are the advantages of putting the helping relationship on a trial basis from the outset? What are additional ways of making the person more comfortable?

3. How does one help a person with low self-esteem?

4. How does one work with a reticent person? With an overly-talkative person?

5. What two guidelines emerge from working with these two types of persons, and others?

12. More Typical Situations

The Ultimate Dimension

In this chapter we will continue what we began in the last, here treating: too much or too little talk of God, the conflict-free life, the self-oppressive spirit, the temptations of the good, always problems, referrals, challenging, overdependence, and healing. We will close with three final observations.

Some people come for spiritual direction and, after the first conversation, never speak of God. They talk about their work, life at home, difficulties they are experiencing in relationships but an awareness of God never appears in what they narrate. By contrast, another type of person person comes for spiritual direction, and talks only about his or her prayer. How should one deal with these?

In the case of the person who never speaks of God, it is a question of feeding back the impression once it crystalizes for you, asking why that is, and dealing with the answer. Such a person can also be helped by certain questions which provoke reflection. For example, the simple question: Where is God in all this? Or, What do you think the call of God is in the situation you describe? Or, Where do you experience God in your ordinary day? Some may never have scrutinized matters in this light. The question makes them think, and their immediate answer is worth paying attention to. Such provocative questions serve a further purpose too. The person carries them away like seeds, and in time they produce their fruits. Discoveries are made between interviews, providing matter for further discussion and growth. People begin to get in touch with the God-dimension in their work, life at home, relationships, and everything else.

With the person too centered on prayer, again feedback is probably the first step. A false spiritual assumption may very well be at work in the life of such a one, namely, that the place of the encounter with God is prayer, and that is where it ends. It may be helpful to develop for this person, either through reading you suggest or by explaining some of the ideas developed in an earlier chapter here, a broader vision of God's presence and activity. A helpful question for reflection might be: Where do you experience God in your ordinary day? If that is not specific enough, it could be sharpened to: Where do you experience God's providence for you in your ordinary life? What gifts or signs of God's care are you aware of in your life? How does God introduce a challenge into your life?

No Drama

Sometimes people come in in whose lives there seems to be very little drama. As session follows session, the story which unfolds is one of business as usual every day—no crises, no doubts, no conflicts with others, no big hopes, no big fears. The helper begins to wonder what, if anything, he or she might be able to do to help this person grow. Crises of various sorts are so typically the real growth times in people's lives.

It is pretty difficult to change either a personality or the pattern of a life. But one can lead toward a deeper spiritual quality in such a life by inviting the person to reflect. What is thematic in your prayer? Since prayer is facing God, and facing God means standing in the truth of your life, this question asks about the habitual themes not just of prayer but of the person's life—the dominant emotions, the largest needs. These then become matters for discussion. Or it might be asked: In what way would you like to grow? Or, Where do you feel the call to growth in your life now? This question calls attention to the fact that life is not stasis but process, that time is precious, that we are never finished but always on the way to the fullness of our selfhood. The question is asking where inside or outside yourself are those dynamisms that would take you beyond the place where you are?

Also helpful for a person like this is some provocative reading, something stimulating or challenging. Of such a person too, whose narrative is always so routine that you have a sense of nothing being transacted, the question might be asked: What are you getting out of our conversations? If the person answers little or nothing, there does not seem to be much reason for going on. Not everybody needs spiritual direction all the time.

If the person makes a convincing answer, on the other hand, it is probably good to continue, even if the relationship is not terribly interesting to the helper.

It's Never Good Enough

There is another type of person who tries too hard and is never satisfied, who is constantly busy with and very hard on him- or herself. Some cannot rejoice in their personal gifts or any of their achievements, but see instead always what is lacking to themselves and everything they do. This is a painful way to live, and unproductive besides. "Which of you by fretting can add a cubit to your span of life?" (Mt 6:27). But this is one of the directions in which spiritual seriousness moves.

This person probably does not know what grace, i.e., God's graciousness, means, and has not yet accepted acceptance. The crucial question here is: What kind of God do you serve? For it seems that God is implicitly understood as judge and slavedriver, and one's whole life is geared to the impossible response. The misconception needs to be pointed out and corrected, on the basis of Jesus' whole way of treating people. Illustrations are abundant in the gospels, and might be suggested as matter for prayer precisely under the aspect of Jesus' unconditional acceptance—in fact, his positive preference for those who were not well (Mt 9:10–13).

It is quite possible that this person thinks of others the way he or she thinks of God: "They value me for what I can do, and are keenly aware of my shortcomings." For often, we think of other people and of God in similar terms. There might also be a carryover in the way they treat other people: "You earn love here; you get what you pay for." This is not the Christian life, whose watchword is: "Be kind to one another, tenderhearted, forgiving one another as God in Christ has forgiven you" (Eph 4:32). "If God has so loved us, we also ought to love one another" (1 Jn 4:11). Helping a person to move from the mentality of justification by works to justification by faith is not a quick or easy operation. What is important is to be alert to the signs of this sort of misconception of the Christian life, a ready trap for good people. Then it is partly a matter of instruction, partly a matter of suggesting texts for prayer and reflection, and very largely a matter of helper as sacrament. You must embody the kind of love you are talking about, the love of unconditional acceptance, valuing the person not on the basis of accomplishments but on the basis of mere human personhood. Your own relationship with God is important too. Is *your* God Father, or is he slavedriver and judge?

Temptations Under the Aspect of Good

What we see in this sort of case is an instance of a more widespread problem in the spiritual life. It is that the temptations of good people are subtle, not gross, and that good people are tempted precisely by what appears to be the moral good. Temptations to obvious evil are not the ones which usually get them. It is rather the subtle and deceptive ones, temptations which do not look like temptations at all but rather like movements toward greater holiness, which take hold of their lives and destroy them. Thus, it is because the person we just considered is a good and spiritually serious person that he or she is striving so hard to please God and be worthy of his love. What shows that the movement is not from God is the fact that it is contrary to the spirit of the gospel and that it works destructively rather than constructively in the life of the person. It works against peace too, putting anxiety in its place. And peace is the sign of the presence of God.

There are a host of such temptations in the lives of good people. Some folks never say No to any request others make of them. Why? Because they are good people and want to be generous. How do we know this is a temptation rather than a movement of God's Spirit? Because it leads to such an overload in the person's life that he or she loses peace and tranquility and is gradually pushed to a nervous breakdown or the abandonment of the apostolate—in a word, destruction. Some people are so concerned about purity of conscience and, in connection with it, integral confession of sins—both laudable things—that they become scrupulous and work themselves up into a terrible state of anxiety over the sacrament of reconciliation. Why do they do it? Not because they are bad people, but because they are good. Their goodness is driven to an extreme and wreaks destruction on them. Again, the sign that this is temptation is that its results are turmoil and sadness, whereas the sign of God's presence and activity is peace, tranquility, joy (Gal 5:22). Some people work so hard to pray and to be fully recollected when they pray, that they get headaches. Here again their goodness works against them.

Some good people get caught in a habit of masturbation, drinking, or fits of laziness which at times defeat their best efforts. So they lacerate themselves interiorly, and this follow-up harms them more than the original actions. They think it is God's judgment under which they stand, but it is really their own judgment wrought upon themselves—self-loathing, self-hatred, self-punishment. God, meanwhile, is patient and forgiving, slow to anger and abounding in kindness and steadfast love (Ex 34:6). They do it because they are good people and want to be perfect for God. God, on the other hand, would be insulted to hear that he is so strangely understood and impersonated.

There are other subtle and deceptive temptations which afflict good folks. There is the temptation to be always self-sufficient and not to be a burden to anyone, to be always the helper and never the one in need. This too, well motivated though it be, works destructively against one, blocking the acceptance of one's full humanity and working against the experience of God's graciousness. The fruits are often loneliness, the maintenance of a baseless pride, the drying up of affectivity, nervous breakdown. Some celibates, well motivated, are so concerned to maintain their celibacy untainted that they touch no one and do not allow anyone even psychic closeness. Fear is the governor here, preventing normal socialization. Fear keeps these people from ever testing the limits of their celibacy and discovering that celibate integrity is quite compatible with warm physical contact and close friendship. Christian celibacy cannot be for the purpose of not loving. It is justifiable in a *Christian* world view only if it makes more love possible. Thus this fear militates against the good, though it presents itself as a holy inspiration. It is another example of the subtle temptations of the spiritually earnest.

Under this category would also fall the choice, through humility, to withhold one's ideas and suggestions and even one's friendship; the clinging, through humility, to elemental forms of prayer when God leads toward more advanced ways; the working oneself to the bone day after day, through generosity, without allowing oneself any time for doing something one would really enjoy. In sum, good people are usually tempted by the moral good itself, but the moral good driven to an extreme where it is no longer the moral good.

Problems Only

When someone consistently talks to the problem side of life, to difficulties in living at home, to one's own moral weakness in a particular regard, to a very trying situation at work, there are two questions which need to be asked. The first is: Can you see any good coming out of all this? The second: What is the call of God to you in this situation ?

The first question tends to surprise people, and that is its value. There are sides of the situation they are not looking at. What good can possibly come out of a losing battle with a moral weakness? Gaining some insight into the quality of God's love, for one. We might previously have thought that one could do whatever one set one's mind to. What good could possibly come out of a tension-filled living situation. The eventual facing of the causes of those tensions, for one, and a confrontation which might be very good for everybody. Growth in personal flexibility and in one's capacity to adapt to a variety of personality types, for another. What good could possibly come from being depressed or lonely for a long period? The gradual development of the dissatisfaction one needs to make costly changes in one's life, for one. The best possible preparation for ministry to the depressed or lonely, for another. What good could possibly come from being criticized or persecuted in one's work? A toughening of the skin, for one, and a growing freedom from the need for approval. Clear evidence that one is in the wrong line of work, for another, or that one takes the wrong approach to it. All these situations of difficulty and struggle, in other words, are growth-inviting situations. They are all instances of the pattern of death/resurrection. The role of the helper is partly to listen and empathize with those who suffer, but partly also to prod them to the kinds of growth these experiences can yield.

That is where the first question meets the second: What is the call of God to you in this situation? For it may not be simply a thing to be endured, but a circumstance which challenges one to action. The first Christian response to evil, Teilhard de Chardin points out, is not resignation but resistance. Only when one has done all one can to resist and overcome evil is it time for resignation, turning the unsolved remainder over to God in trust. The call of God in oppressive circumstances is not always to grin and bear it. What would Jesus do in my situation? Would he endure? Would he confront? Would he comfort? Would he take action to heal? Would he walk away? He did all of these, according to circumstances.

Referrals

How do you deal with a person who needs to be referred to a professional psychotherapist? It requires some delicacy. You do not want to say after one conversation: What you need is psychotherapy. Take more time, waiting both for your impression to become more sure and for the other to know that you have heard and that you do care for him or her. Then make the suggestion gently and with obvious personal concern, preferably also with a competent therapist in mind in whom you have confidence. People need to be helped to understand that you are not dropping or rejecting them, and that you do not think they are crazy. Many seek therapy today not because they cannot cope but because they desire deeper self-understanding or some help in working through a chronic source of stress. There should be no stigma attached to that. Put your recommendation in the form of a suggestion or a question, not of a final conclusion: "Have you ever considered . . ." or, "I wonder how you would feel about trying . . . ." Then give your reasons for suggesting it.

The helper should be aware of the limits of psychotherapy. People can go a long time and spend a lot of money without making significant progress. There are no easy answers to deep human problems, no quick cures. Given the ability to convey love and to understand and deal with ordinary human psychodynamics, you yourself may be able to walk as well as a professional counselor with someone going through a painful process of growth. The basic judgment that has to be made is whether you are dealing with something that is over your head or not. Usually your gut will tell you.

If you do make a referral, does this mean the end of your relationship? There is no reason why it should, if you and the therapist are not working at cross purposes. Your main concern is still spiritual growth, a concern the therapist may not share at all but which the client still wants. For the question always remains: Where is God in the experience you are going through? If the helper is not doing psychotherapy, and doing it in a very different way than the therapist is, there should be no conflict. It will, of course, be helpful to your efforts as spiritual director if you are informed from time to time how things are going with the therapist and what sorts of issues are being worked on. The therapist may be similarly interested in what you are doing.

As an alternative to one-on-one therapy in certain cases, group therapy merits a serious look. It often proves to be more effective. Particularly for individuals who are poorly socialized (lonely, unable to make friends), for those who need a support group on a particular struggle (divorced, alcoholic, overweight), for those who love to analyze and talk about themselves indefinitely without changing anything, for those who would profit from interaction with peers in a situation of honest feedback, the group setting has marked advantages over the one-on-one. Each case has to be judged on its own merits.

Deciding what you can handle yourself and what you would do better to refer to a professional counselor is a matter of balancing your own limitations against the limitations of professional counselors, and your own strengths against the strengths of professional counselors. There are very gifted people in the field of professional counseling, people who not only have the basic personal gifts but an extraordinary refinement of them in skills of proven effectiveness. Referring someone to such a person for help on a chronic problem may be the finest service you can render. Referring a person with an acute problem may avert disaster. On the other hand, there are unhelpful counselors complete with degrees and licenses, and there are the inevitable limitations of all helping efforts where human problems are concerned. In the end, it comes down to a prudential judgment. A lot depends on the problem in question, on the person to whom you would make the referral, and on what you feel capable of doing yourself.

How Challenging?

If you are working with people who usually take the initiative and bring the agenda, watch, among other things, what they always talk about and what they never talk about. It might be helpful to them at some point if you reflect this back. It may tell them where they are in a rut, and what areas of growth they are blind to or may not want to look at.

This raises the question of how "challenging" a spiritual director should be. Should you be aggressive? Should you push people, or call them to account? Should you tell them what is wrong with them? It depends mostly on the sort of person you are dealing with. Some people want this type of thing, and will ask for it in the initial interview. "I want you to challenge me." Or, "I want you to be firm with me, call me to task, give me a kick in the pants." A larger number of people, it seems, are more in need of being accepted and encouraged. They are hard enough on themselves, and do not need to be told by someone else that they are not measuring up. Yet they are usually open to suggestions, or to questions which make them think. In dealing with the generally sensitive and fragile human being, it seems to be a greater danger that one will break the bruised reed than that one will fail to be sufficiently challenging. This is not to say there is no place for it.

Overdependence

What about overdependence? It usually will not develop if the helper does not allow it to. It is resisted simply by keeping responsibility for decision where it belongs, by not agreeing to needlessly frequent meetings and by giving honest feedback. The task does not end with resisting and refusing. Its term is the building of confidence in the others, the convincing them that they can themselves be responsible and live good lives. Lead toward more autonomy. Confirm whatever you can confirm.

Can you be spiritual director to your close friend? First of all, you probably already are, for good or ill, without the title. Friends influence one another a great deal as they talk things over, offering spontaneous reactions. But two friends can make this intent more explicit. One asks the other to act as spiritual director, and during a given hour does not just gab randomly, but takes as serious spiritual stock of him- or herself before the other as would be appropriate in a more formal setting This sometimes works well. There are a couple of prerequisites for success. The first is that the person so designated really have something to offer the other. When the blind lead the blind, they don't do too well. The other is that the person so designated can really be objective with his or her friend. Love at times can blur the vision, or make one too kind. For these reasons, over and above all that one gains from a friend, one might well wish to ask someone else to serve as one's spiritual director.

What if your client falls in love with you? Well, such a development is really not so surprising if the relationship is going well. You obviously care for the person, are someone with whom he or she can talk openly and freely about deep personal concerns, and may have proved to be extraordinarily helpful in hard times. Strong feelings naturally develop. Genuine love on both sides need not work against the relationship at all, but might positively assist it. If this love moves to really being "in love" and is mutual, you have a different situation. You are probably no longer doing spiritual direction, and together you will have to work out what you want to do with the relationship.

If, on the other hand, you, the director, are not in love with the other, though he or she is with you, you can continue to do direction, and the working through of the other person's feelings might be very growthful for him or her. It is important that the feelings of both be out in the open in this situation. If there is honesty and a mutual quest of the good, there is a real opportunity for self knowledge, the acceptance of one's feelings, communication and negotiation, maturation and growth. If the situation is reversed, and the director has very strong feelings for the client, it is usually not helpful to the relationship to unload these feelings on the client. It is not what he or she came for. For one's own part, the feelings are not to be fought down or denied. They are not bad, and are usually manageable. You can often work them through yourself, or do it with the help of someone else.

Healing

We become aware sometimes that the person sitting before us has been deeply wounded by some experience, and is in need of healing. Unless the experience is healed, the person will remain stuck there, or at least permanently impaired.

In raising the question of healing at this point, we are not introducing a brand new subject. All Christian helping relationships are healing in some degree. The forgiveness of sins heals. The experience of acceptance heals. Love and care heal. Ordinary healing takes place, in other words, in all helping relationships, whether this is explicitly adverted to or not.

There is, over and above this, a process which can be used to bring the healing of a painful memory. The literature on this and other kinds of healing is extensive today. We offer the briefest summary of an approach to the healing of a crippling memory.

Any experience can be either a blessing or a curse, depending very largely on how one views it. An experience is a painful memory because one is preoccupied with the evil side of it. The first step in healing it is discovering its good side. The helper assists the other in naming any and all benefits which have come from the painful experience—e.g., growth in one's relationship with God, the development of compassion, preparation for ministry through deepened understanding of a particular sort of human affliction. These are the sorts of things we called attention to above in dealing with the person who sees only the problem side of life.

Healing a painful memory next demands the forgiveness of the person who caused the hurt. This is an essential part of letting the memory go, but frequently it is very difficult. The wounded person needs help here in understanding the offender better. What was that person's background? What pressures might have been present at the time of the incident? What was the buildup? Would I have done better in the same circumstances? Have I done better in my own? Then there is need to turn to the Lord for healing. One prays for help in forgiving and letting this obsession go. One asks to be freed of the burden. One petitions that one's narrow understanding and one's heart of stone be replaced by the broadmindedness and compassion of the Lord. Some meditation on Jesus' ways of dealing with his own hurts, with those who sinned against him, with those he found in pain at the hands of others, can be helpful here. This part of the healing process is greatly strengthened by praying together. The helper might lay hands on the other's head, or join hands facing him or her in a sitting position, that the two might join their prayers for the Lord's healing.

We need to recognize that some human problems are beyond our power to solve. The finest counseling and the warmest unconditional love are not enough sometimes to heal people of the wounds which maim them, or to free them from the destructive habits which hold them bound. Christian helping relationships are always contextualized in faith, and a power greater than ourselves is ever at work in them. But sometimes it is particularly fitting to call directly on the power of God for healing and liberation.

Three Final Observations

Prayer in helping sessions has broader usefulness than the one just named. It is not an absolute requirement, since it can safely be presumed that prayer on both sides surrounds the relationship. Yet some moments of prayer together might be very helpful, whether at the beginning or end or at some critical juncture in the session. It makes clear that this relationship is indeed in God and is dependent on God for its fruitfulness, and it asks for help where help is looked for. It can be a real assist to the person seeking counsel, strengthening him or her to face issues that need to be faced and to be honest about them. There are sometimes moments in the midst of an exchange where the need for prayer is particularly felt. Whoever feels it should be free to suggest it. It might be spoken prayer. It could just as well be some moments of shared silence.

Have a box of kleenex on hand. People cry. A box of kleenex

on the table tells them that other people cry too, and that it is OK to cry here. Let it happen. In fact, you might add a word which assures the person starting to cry that that is perfectly acceptable.

Take care about confidentiality. What people tell you about themselves is a sacred trust. If you feel the need to consult someone about a case you are dealing with, ask the client's permission. It will usually be given, and the consultation can be done in such a way that anonymity is preserved. Aside from this, silence is golden.

QUESTIONS FOR REFLECTION AND DISCUSSION

1. In dealing with those who never speak of God, yet come for spiritual direction, what sorts of questions might you ask to provoke faith-reflection?

2. How would you deal with someone who spoke only of prayer?

3. How might you deal with someone coming regularly but having very little to report or discuss?

4. How might you help someone who serves a judging, driving God?

5. What are some of the subtle temptations (deceptions) of good people?

6. How do you move a person from a mere reporting of woes to something more constructive?

7. What is the cue that tells you you should refer someone to a professional therapist, and what are some of things to keep in mind when you do?

8. Is it the role of the Christian helper to challenge the other to growth?

9. How would you handle a developing overdependence, or a falling in love, or a request from a close friend to be his or her spiritual director?

10. How would you deal with someone you saw to be paralyzed around a painful memory?

11. What other typical situations do you find it diffcult to deal with?

SUGGESTIONS FOR FURTHER READING

St. Ignatius Loyola   "Rules for the Discernment of Spirits" in *The Spiritual Exercises*

Francis MacNutt   *Healing*

Dennis and Matthew Linn   *Healing Life's Hurts*

13. The Gift of the Needy

Carl Jung once remarked that all the really great conversations of his life had been with nameless people. As his reputation grew, he was increasingly invited into the circles of the powerful and shared their conversation. But his retrospect on the really deep and satisfying exchanges of his life revealed to him that they were almost all with anonymous men and women who had opened their hearts to him and shown him something of the richness of their inner selves.

This book has been about the work of the Christian helper, the helper's desire to be sacrament for another person, the helper's efforts to listen perceptively and, by giving appropriate responses, to help people to fuller lives in Christ. The accent has been on giving and helping. Now it is time to say something about what the helper receives and how he or she is helped.

There is a saying of Jesus about giving and receiving, and its paradox is well realized in the economy in which Christian helping take place. He says:

Give, and they will give to you; good measure, pressed down, shaken together, and running over, they will pour into your lap. For the measure you use with others they in turn will use with you (Lk 6:38).

It is a strange thing, but the big winner in helping relationships is the helper, and usually the person who sought help has not the slightest idea this enrichment has occurred. I have experienced it again and again. The helper may be sacrament; the person helped is certainly sacrament too. The helper may somehow challenge the other to grow; the person seeking help certainly challenges me to grow.

The basic thing the person seeking help sacramentalizes is Christ in need. He comes in weakness and distress, calling to our compassion, generosity, gifts of healing. We may not always recognize that it is Christ, but this is not an uncommon oversight. It is conspicuous in Matthew's last judgment scene:

> Lord, when did we see you hungry and feed you, or thirsty and give you drink.... And the king will answer them, "Truly, I say to you, as you did it to one of the least of these my brothers or sisters, you did it to me" (Mt 25:37–40).

Christ has identified himself with his poor, suffering, needy members, whether we recognize that it is he or not. It is our privilege to serve him there. But in those who come to us for help, it is more than the suffering of Christ that shows. His goodness is revealed in them too. Even as they confess their sins, failings, and weaknesses, their goodness shines out the more eloquently. Again and again I have found it a privilege to be let into the hearts of people, there in the personal center where the battle between good and evil is being fought, the crucifixion is going on, the crucial choices of life are being made. It is a place of pain for people; it is also a beautiful place. It is a kind of temple, and so often I have stood in awe inside it. There is where the mystery of God meets the mystery of the human person, and faith, hope, and love struggle to win out over unbelief, despair, and selfishness. I have yet to meet someone in whom the former things were not winning, though the cost at times is great and the heat of the battle obscures the results where the warrior is concerned.

I have been with people who bear heavier burdens than I bear, and carry them more gracefully. I have talked with people earnestly seeking things I have slacked off in my quest of, and I have been prodded to renew the effort. I have listened to people living a much more vibrant faith. Folks have knocked me out with an immediate, unconditional trust, which I have wanted to emulate. In others I have been shown the meaning of thankfulness as an habitual attitude to life. Repeatedly I have beheld in wonder the mystery of God's dealing with the individual, the infinitely varied avenues of his self-manifestation, the subtlety and the gentleness, the slow pacing of the invitation, the surprise gift, the late conversion, the unexpected healing, the highpoints of a life-long relationship. And usually I have been stirred by the wholeheartedness of the person's response.

The joy of the helper is the joy of being utilized. "You really helped me," someone says. "I don't understand quite how it happened," I say, "but nothing could make me happier than to have helped you." What could be more satisfying than to lighten a burden, to show a way through, to draw out a meaning present in a situation but overlooked, a meaning that makes all the difference? What is more satisfying than to affirm the good in another, to confirm what is already well conceived and under fine execution, to show lonely persons that someone else cares and to see them experience not only you but God himself in the fellowship? Is it not being able to do things like this for others that makes life worth living?

I am not fond of being interrupted, and the caller does interrupt. But people who come usually teach me more than the book I was reading, and give me deeper satisfaction than I would otherwise have found. I don't enjoy being worked to death, but some of the days I have gone to bed most exhausted have been days I have gone to bed happiest, amazed at how rich the day has been in people. Some made me feel better about my own weaknesses by showing me that I am not the only one. Some have brought a powerful presence of God to me. Some have shown me how good I have it. Some have stimulated me to think, to try to find more adequate approaches to important human questions and needs. They have sent me to prayer, keenly aware that help must come from beyond myself. They have told me what my gifts are, and encouraged me to keep using them. They have taught me humility and the wonder of God's economy, an economy in which an earthen vessel like myself can be a helper. They have convinced and reconvinced me that life is people or it is nothing, and that amazing things can happen when one human being takes a chance and opens him- or herself to another.

A picture of the world is given every day in the paper or on the evening news. There we see the less savory aspects of the human scene—the robberies, killings, and frauds, the disputes, the strikes, and the wars. The helper contemplates a different scene, the terrain of the individual soul. And he or she begins to understand why, in spite of all that the newspapers and television have to report, God so loved the world that he sent his only Son.

QUESTIONS FOR REFLECTION AND DISCUSSION

Call to mind some of the people you have helped over the years. How have they gifted you? Perhaps you would want to make this the subject of some prayer of thanksgiving, or of some sharing, or both.